Utilize este código QR para se cadastrar de forma mais rápida:

Ou, se preferir, entre em:
www.richmond.com.br/ac/livroportal

e siga as instruções para ter acesso aos conteúdos exclusivos do **Portal e Livro Digital**

CÓDIGO DE ACESSO:

A 00026 PEACE2E 2 93205

Faça apenas um cadastro. Ele será válido para:

Da semente ao livro,
sustentabilidade por todo o caminho

Plantar florestas
A madeira que serve de matéria-prima para nosso papel vem de plantio renovável, ou seja, não é fruto de desmatamento. Essa prática gera milhares de empregos para agricultores e ajuda a recuperar áreas ambientais degradadas.

Fabricar papel e imprimir livros
Toda a cadeia produtiva do papel, desde a produção de celulose até a encadernação do livro, é certificada, cumprindo padrões internacionais de processamento sustentável e boas práticas ambientais.

Criar conteúdos
Os profissionais envolvidos na elaboração de nossas soluções educacionais buscam uma educação para a vida pautada por curadoria editorial, diversidade de olhares e responsabilidade socioambiental.

Construir projetos de vida
Oferecer uma solução educacional Moderna é um ato de comprometimento com o futuro das novas gerações, possibilitando uma relação de parceria entre escolas e famílias na missão de educar!

Apoio:
www.twosides.org.br

Fotografe o Código QR e conheça melhor esse caminho.
Saiba mais em *moderna.com.br/sustentavel*

Students for PEACE

Eduardo Amos
Renata Condi

2

Student's Book & Workbook

Richmond

Richmond

Direção editorial: Sandra Possas

Edição executiva de inglês: Izaura Valverde
Edição executiva de produção e multimídia: Adriana Pedro de Almeida

Coordenação de arte: Raquel Buim
Coordenação de revisão: Rafael Spigel

Edição de texto: Ludmila De Nardi, Nathália Horvath
Assistência editorial: Angela Cristina Costa Neves, Cíntia Afarelli Pereira, Leila Scatena
Elaboração de conteúdo: Beatriz Nosé, Christiane Araújo, Cristina Mayer, Doris Soares, Luciana Silva
Preparação de originais: Helaine Albuquerque, Roberta Moratto Risther
Revisão: Carolina Waideman, Flora Manzione, Gabriele Martin Cândido, Gislaine Caprioli Costa, Kandy Saraiva, Katia Gouveia Vitale, Márcio Martins, Marina de Andrade, Vivian Cristina de Souza

Projeto gráfico: Carol Duran
Edição de arte: Fabiane Eugenio
Diagramação: Amaiscom
Capa: Carol Duran
Criações: Anderson Sunakozawa, Camila Ranelli, Fabiane Eugenio, Mateus Banti

Website: Daniela Carrete, Frodo Almeida (*design*)
Social Media: Ana Paula Campos, Priscila Oliveira Vieira (edição de conteúdo); Eloah Cristina (analista de projetos); Altair Sampaio, Frodo Almeida (*design*)
Digital Hub: Ana Paula Campos, Priscila Oliveira Vieira (edição de conteúdo); Eloah Cristina (analista de projetos); Daniela Carrete (*design*)
PEACE Builders: Ana Paula Campos (edição de conteúdo); Daniela Carrete (*design*)
Digital Academy: Gabrielle Navarro, Thaís Teixeira Tardivo (edição de conteúdo); Daniel Favalli (coordenação de produção); Angela Urbinatti, Mônica M. Oldrine (*design*)
Novo Portal Educacional Richmond: Sheila Rizzi (edição)
Livro Digital Interativo: Gabrielle Navarro, Thaís Teixeira Tardivo (edição de conteúdo); Daniel Favalli (coordenação de produção); Angela Urbinatti (*design*)

Iconografia: Marcia Sato, Sara Alencar
Coordenação de *bureau*: Rubens M. Rodrigues
Tratamento de imagens: Fernando Bertolo, Joel Aparecido, Luiz Carlos Costa, Marina M. Buzzinaro
Pré-impressão: Alexandre Petreca, Everton L. de Oliveira, Márcio H. Kamoto, Vitória Sousa
Áudio: Maximal Studio

Todos os *sites* mencionados nesta obra foram reproduzidos apenas para fins didáticos. A Richmond não tem controle sobre seu conteúdo, o qual foi cuidadosamente verificado antes de sua utilização.
Websites mentioned in this material were quoted for didactic purposes only. Richmond has no control over their content and urges care when using them.

Embora todas as medidas tenham sido tomadas para identificar e contatar os detentores de direitos autorais sobre os materiais reproduzidos nesta obra, isso nem sempre foi possível. A editora estará pronta a retificar quaisquer erros dessa natureza assim que notificada.
Every effort has been made to trace the copyright holders, but if any omission can be rectified, the publishers will be pleased to make the necessary arrangements.

Impressão e acabamento: Coan Indústria Gráfica Ltda.
Lote: 284780 / 284781

Créditos das fotos: Capa: RadomanDurkovic/iStockphoto; p. 6: MyImages - Micha/Shutterstock, pixelliebe/iStockphoto, GuoZhongHua/Shutterstock, MyImages - Micha/Shutterstock, James R. Martin/Shutterstock, hidesy/Shutterstock, Africa Studio/Shutterstock, Yuganov Konstantin/Shutterstock; p. 8: Yalana/iStockphoto, monkeybusinessimages/iStockphoto; p. 9: EvgeniyShkolenko/iStockphoto, OHishiapply/Shutterstock, Cavan Images/Getty Images; p. 10: Highwaystarz-Photography/iStockphoto, Steve Debenport/iStockphoto, tofang/Shutterstock, Antonio_Diaz/iStockphoto; p. 12: Kentucky Virtual Library; p. 13: oatawa/iStockphoto, Eva-Katalin/iStockphoto, shahfarshid/iStockphoto, Daviles/iStockphoto, fizkes/iStockphoto; p. 14: Common Sense Media; p. 16: BigMouse/Shutterstock; p. 20: DannyRM/iStockphoto, ArtMarie/iStockphoto; p. 21: Cesar Diniz/Pulsar Imagens, Bartek Zyczynski/Shutterstock, THEPALMER/iStockphoto; p. 22: nicoolay/iStockphoto; p. 25: © 2018 Washington Post, © 2014 Bob Weber Jr. & Jay Stephens/Dist. by Andrews McMeel Syndication; p. 26: ©2018 King Features Syndicate/Ipress; p. 27: nalinratphi/iStockphoto, karelnoppe/Shutterstock, mediaphotos/iStockphoto, View Apart/Shutterstock, kali9/iStockphoto, gehringj/iStockphoto, PeopleImages/iStockphoto, zeljkosantrac/iStockphoto; p. 28: Reprodução; p. 30: vtmila/iStockphoto; p. 33: Nokuro/Shutterstock; p. 34: renatalang/iStockphoto, katclay/iStockphoto, Bartosz Hadyniak/iStockphoto; p. 35: DOUGBERRY/iStockphoto, gyro/iStockphoto, Ababsolutum/iStockphoto; p. 36: Pavel L Photo and Video/Shutterstock, AJ_Watt/iStockphoto, jacoblund/iStockphoto, MOLIVARES1/iStockphoto; p. 38: Billion Photos/Shutterstock, urbancow/iStockphoto, MaksimYremenko/iStockphoto; p. 39: CherriesJD/iStockphoto, Sadeugra/iStockphoto, PeopleImages/iStockphoto, WestLight/iStockphoto, scanrail/iStockphoto, Jane1e/iStockphoto; p. 41: Africa Studio/Shutterstock, Ridofranz/iStockphoto, zhudifeng/iStockphoto, petrograd99/iStockphoto, KatarzynaBialasiewicz/iStockphoto; p. 42: Viorel Sima/Shutterstock, grafvision/Shutterstock, MaFelipe/iStockphoto, Nkarol/iStockphoto; p. 43: Sandrine Huet/Le Pictorium/Alamy/Fotoarena, Bygone Collection/Alamy Stock Photo, pidjoe/iStockphoto, aydinmutlu/iStockphoto; p. 44: Alfredo Allais/iStockphoto; p. 46: karandaev/iStockphoto, Elena_Danileiko/iStockphoto, MSPhotographic/iStockphoto; p. 47: trindade51s/iStockphoto, TinaFields/iStockphoto, margouillatphotos/iStockphoto; p. 48: Harvard University; p. 49: littleclie/iStockphoto, VankaD/iStockphoto; p. 50: xxmmxx/iStockphoto, Ann_Zhuravleva/iStockphoto, chas53/iStockphoto, brunorbs/iStockphoto, ehaurylik/iStockphoto, nitrub/iStockphoto, pilipphoto/iStockphoto, fcafotodigital/iStockphoto, Kuvona/iStockphoto; p. 54: gustavomellossa/iStockphoto, Global_Pics/iStockphoto, Freestocker/iStockphoto, ESOlex/iStockphoto; p. 56: Dean Drobot/Shutterstock; p. 58: Martina Bocchio/Awakening/Alamy/Fotoarena; p. 60: Baptiste Giroudon/Paris Match/Getty Images, baranozdemir/iStockphoto; p. 61: dolgachov/iStockphoto, LightFieldStudios/iStockphoto; p. 65: DFree/Shutterstock, André Horta/Fotoarena, Fabio Teixeira/Anadolu Agency/Getty Images, Oleg Golovnev/Shutterstock; p. 66: DaveAlan/iStockphoto, SSPL/Getty Images, Sinisha Karich/Shutterstock, axelbueckert/iStockphoto, graja/Shutterstock, Dio5050/iStockphoto; p. 67: Stardust; p. 68: Victor Dolabaille/Shutterstock, Tinxi/Shutterstock, OlegDoroshin/Shutterstock, vm/iStockphoto; p. 69: Beto Celli; p. 72: DINODIA/Alamy/Fotoarena, Acervo Ultima Hora/Folhapress; p. 73: Photo12/Universal Images Group/Getty Images, Chris Jackson/Getty Images, Bettmann/Getty Images, Hulton Archive/Getty Images; p. 74: Simon Spotlight, Penguin; p. 75: Album/akg-images/Pictures From History/Fotoarena; p. 77: I AM JANE GOODALL by Brad Meltzer, copyright © 2016 by Forty-Four; p. 79. Album/akg-images/Fotoarena; p. 80: Penguin; p. 82: MaskaRad/iStockphoto; p. 84: Diamond Films, BBC Films; p. 85: Fox 2000 Pictures; p. 86: cifotart/iStockphoto, Gerson Gerloff/Pulsar Imagens, dabldy/iStockphoto, Carlos Moura/CB/D.A Press; p. 88: American Museum of Natural History, New York; p. 91: vbacarin/iStockphoto, Vitoriano Jr/iStockphoto, bcorreabh/iStockphoto, VanessaVolk/iStockphoto, Iuoman/iStockphoto, fotoVoyager/iStockphoto; p. 92: Colleen Jenkins/Reuters/Fotoarena; p. 94: National Archives of Australia, fotofritz16/iStockphoto, Lonely Planet Images/Getty Images; p. 98: SolStock/iStockphoto, Caftor/iStockphoto, wundervisuals/iStockphoto, skynesher/iStockphoto, BraunS/iStockphoto; p. 100: Saiyna Bashir/Reuters/Fotoarena; p. 105: diego_cervo/iStockphoto, SerrNovik/iStockphoto, Africa Studio/Shutterstock, Ridofranz/iStockphoto, diego_cervo/iStockphoto, IPGGutenbergUKLtd/iStockphoto; p. 106: AfricaImages/iStockphoto, EvgeniiAnd/iStockphoto, Zabavna/iStockphoto, manley099/iStockphoto, RyanJLane/iStockphoto, shironosov/iStockphoto; p. 110: duncan1890/iStockphoto, Historia/Shutterstock, ZU_09/iStockphoto; p. 114: Neydtstock/iStockphoto, gregory_lee/iStockphoto, urfinguss/iStockphoto, orinoco-art/iStockphoto; p. 115: xavier gallego Morell/Shutterstock; p. 116: ahavelaar/iStockphoto, monkeybusinessimages/iStockphoto, Marta_Kent/iStockphoto, Viktor Drachev/Getty Images, AndreyKaderov/iStockphoto, Imgorthand/iStockphoto; p. 117: foto da Batrawy; p. 118: nicolesy/iStockphoto, DMEPhotography/iStockphoto, PeopleImages/iStockphoto, Rawpixel.com/Shutterstock, RomanBabakin/iStockphoto; p. 119: TheCrimsonMonkey/iStockphoto; p. 120: Marat Musabirov/iStockphoto, ddsign_stock/iStockphoto, ArxOnt/iStockphoto, juffy/iStockphoto, Paperkites/iStockphoto, ValentynVolkov/iStockphoto, vetkit/iStockphoto, rocksunderwater/iStockphoto, scope-xl/iStockphoto, Dzurag/iStockphoto; p. 121: Chris Willson/Alamy/Fotoarena, Porames Rojanatreekoon/Alamy/Fotoarena, Stefan Sollfors/Alamy/Fotoarena, Yoshikazu TSUNO/AFP, Oleksiy Maksymenko/Alamy/Fotoarena, James Leynse/Corbis/Getty Images, Zeynep Demir/Shutterstock, Hal_P/Shutterstock; p. 123: Uncle Leo/Shutterstock; p. 124: Bettmann/Getty Images; p. 125: Razvan/iStockphoto; p. 126: Lehnartz/iStockphoto, Topical Press Agency/Getty Images, Keystone-France/Gamma-Keystone/Getty Images, Keystone-France/Gamma-Rapho/Getty Images; p. 127: Twin Desgin/Shutterstock, NurPhoto/Getty Images, Bilanol/Shutterstock, Hung Chung Chih/Shutterstock; p. 128: Steve Debenport/iStockphoto, SolStock/iStockphoto, Ridofranz/iStockphoto; p. 142: Penguin Books, Warner Bros Pictures, The Con; p. 143: Little, Brown Books for Young Learners, Back Bay Books.

Dados Internacionais de Catalogação na Publicação (CIP)
(Câmara Brasileira do Livro, SP, Brasil)

Amos, Eduardo
   Students for peace / Eduardo Amos, Renata Condi. -
- 2. ed. -- São Paulo : Moderna, 2019. -- (Students
for peace)

   Obra em 4 v. do 6º ao 9º ano.

   1. Inglês (Ensino fundamental) I. Condi, Renata.
II. Título. III. Série.

19-26387   CDD-372.652

Índices para catálogo sistemático:
1. Inglês : Ensino fundamental   372.652
Maria Paula C. Riyuzo - Bibliotecária - CRB-8/7639

ISBN 978-85-16-12050-4 (LA)
ISBN 978-85-16-12051-1 (LP)

Reprodução proibida. Art. 184 do Código Penal e Lei 9.610 de 19 de fevereiro de 1998.

Todos os direitos reservados.

RICHMOND
EDITORA MODERNA LTDA.
Rua Padre Adelino, 758 – Belenzinho
São Paulo – SP – Brasil – CEP 03303-904
www.richmond.com.br
2019

Impresso no Brasil

Dear student,

This is **Students for PEACE** – a set of materials designed not only to help you learn English, but also to make you think about, discuss and act upon important issues related to your life and your community. **Students for PEACE** is the result of many years of study and research.

When we first sat down to write this series, we felt that we had to go beyond the study of the English language because there was something the world needed desperately – peace. And it still needs it. So we decided to make peace education the core of this series and its goal. The ideas presented in **Students for PEACE** are based on the positive concept of peace as justice, tolerance and respect.

This series will certainly help you learn English, but we hope it will also help you understand and acknowledge human diversity and live with one another in harmony, facing the different challenges of the world around you.

As those famous song lyrics said, "All we are saying is give peace a chance!"

Have a nice year!

Editorial team

Scope & sequence

Welcome Chapter (p. 6) — We would like to invite you to create your Students for PEACE profile

	Goals	Explore & Studio	Building blocks & Toolbox	Sync – Listening & Sync – Speaking
1 Going online (p. 8)	• Conduct an oral survey on internet habits. • Explore and write a tutorial. • Explore audios about internet habits. • Explore research and study tools. • Recognize vocabulary related to gadgets. • Understand the uses of the present simple.	• Tutorial	• Gadgets • Present simple (review)	• Internet habits • Presentation of a survey
2 Expression (p. 20)	• Explore written poems. • Recite a poem. • Recognize different kinds of artistic expression. • Take part in discussions about kinds of artistic expression. • Understand a recited poem. • Understand and use the modal verb "can" to describe abilities in the present. • Write a *haiku*.	• Poem • *Haiku*	• Expressions • "Can"/"Can't"	• Poetry slam • Poetry soirée
Peace talk (p. 32)	Be yourself			
3 Meet my culture (p. 34)	• Conduct an interview. • Explore, discuss and learn to respect cultural differences. • Identify the pronoun that replaces the object in a sentence. • Recognize vocabulary related to clothes and accessories. • Understand a written interview with an exchange student. • Understand an oral interview with participants of a cultural event. • Understand and use *wh-* words.	• Interview • Interview transcript	• Clothes and accessories • *Wh-* words, subject and object pronouns	• An interview at an event • Interviewing someone
4 Food and nutrition (p. 46)	• Distinguish between countable and uncountable nouns. • Learn vocabulary related to food. • Read and create a cooking recipe. • Read and understand a text with nutritional information. • Understand an audio with suggestions for a healthy diet. • Understand and use adverbs of frequency to talk about eating habits. • Understand and use the imperative in recipe instructions.	• Recipe	• Adverbs of frequency and food vocabulary • Imperative, countable and uncountable nouns	• *The Dietary Guidelines for the Brazilian Population* • Presenting a recipe
Peace talk (p. 58)	People who eat together stay together			

	Goals	Explore & Studio	Building blocks & Toolbox	Sync – Listening & Sync – Speaking
5 **Entertainment** (p. 60)	• Discuss different forms of entertainment. • Explore and create a timeline. • Identify the use of the prepositions of time "in", "on" and "at". • Recognize the different pronunciations of regular verbs in the past (-ed). • Understand an audio in which people react to some technology from the past. • Use the past simple to understand and create oral and written texts.	• Timeline	• Old technology for entertainment • Past simple of regular verbs	• Participants' reaction to a game • An interactive presentation about entertainment
6 **People and their stories** (p. 72)	• Explore and write a biography. • Identify the use of connectors that express addition, contrast, time, cause and consequence. • Produce an oral biographical narrative. • Reflect on the life stories of people who made a difference because of their contributions to important causes. • Understand a biographical narrative from an audiobook. • Understand and use the past simple of irregular verbs.	• Biography	• Connectors (linking words) • Past simple of irregular verbs	• An audiobook extract • A biographical narrative
Peace talk (p. 84)	Once upon a real time...			
7 **History is all around us** (p. 86)	• Explore encyclopedia entries. • Recognize different kinds of landmarks. • Think about the importance of history. • Understand and create an oral narrative. • Understand and use the past continuous to describe events that were in progress at a certain time in the past. • Write an encyclopedia entry.	• Encyclopedia entry	• Landmarks • Past continuous	• Immigration • A narrative about people and their history
8 **When I was a kid** (p. 98)	• Explore and write a blog post. • Review and contrast the use of the past simple and the past continuous. • Review some connectors. • Talk about different kinds of games. • Understand and share childhood memories. • Understand and use the modal verb "could" to describe abilities in the past. • Understand and use "used to" to talk about habits in the past.	• Blog post	• Games • Past simple, past continuous and "could"	• What's your favorite childhood memory? • My childhood
Peace talk (p. 110)	Moral of the story			

Self-assessment 112	Language reference 130	Glossary 140	References 144
Workbook 113	Interdisciplinary project 134	Learning more 142	
Irregular verbs list 129	Transcripts 137	Track list 144	

Welcome to Students for PEACE!

We would like to invite you to create your Students for PEACE profile

1. Let's create your Students for PEACE profile! Follow the path and write your answer to each question in the space provided.
2. Now, share your profile with your classmates.
3. In groups, talk more about how you change the world. Consider these questions.
   a. What do you do as a group?
   b. What could you do as a group?

A WHAT IS YOUR NAME?

G WHAT ARE YOUR HOBBIES?

H HOW DO YOU CHANGE THE WORLD?

B HOW OLD ARE YOU?

C WHERE DO YOU LIVE?

STUDENTS FOR PEACE PROFILE

D DO YOU HAVE ANY BROTHERS OR SISTERS?

E WHERE DO YOU STUDY?

FRIENDS

F WHAT IS YOUR FAVORITE SUBJECT AT SCHOOL?

1 Going online

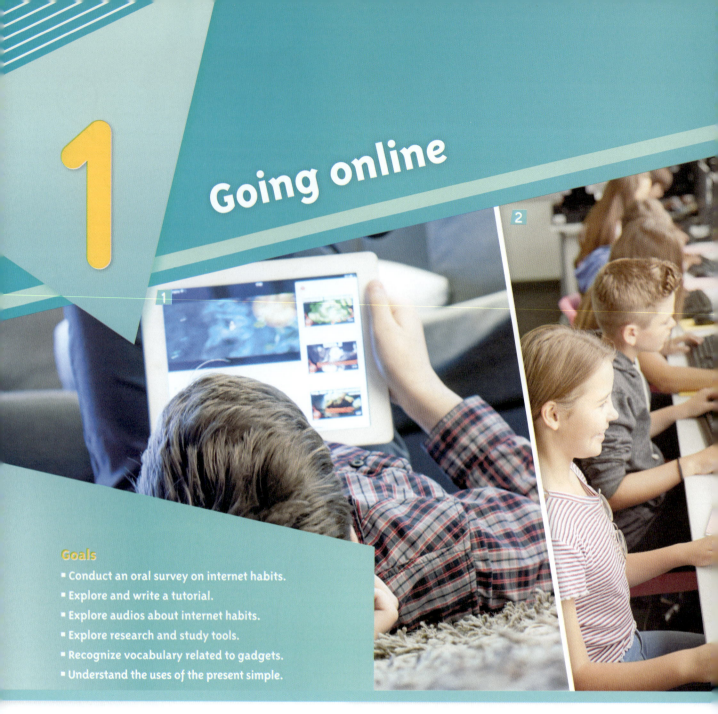

Goals
- Conduct an oral survey on internet habits.
- Explore and write a tutorial.
- Explore audios about internet habits.
- Explore research and study tools.
- Recognize vocabulary related to gadgets.
- Understand the uses of the present simple.

Spark

1 Which picture shows someone or people...

a ☐ making a video?
b ☐ doing research?
c ☐ watching a video?
d ☐ trying to find their way?
e ☐ playing a game?

2 Check all the activities that can be done without internet connection.

a ☐ Play a game.
b ☐ Upload a file.
c ☐ Watch a movie.
d ☐ Do research.
e ☐ Download music.
f ☐ Make a video.

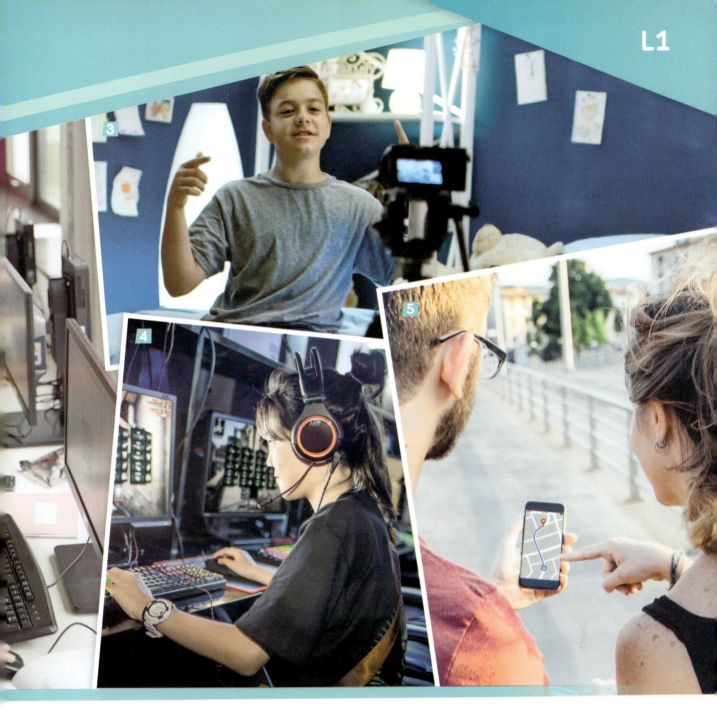

Language clue

☁⬇ **Download** is the transfer of something (video, movie, music, picture, file, software) to a device (computer, cell phone, tablet) using the internet.

☁⬆ **Upload** is the transfer of something (video, movie, music, picture, file, software) from a device (computer, cell phone, tablet) to another using the internet.

3 Some activities can be done both online and offline. Which ones do you prefer doing online?

L1

Explore Tutorial

Pre-reading

1 Look at the pictures. They all relate to tutorials. What could be the title to each tutorial?

> How to apply makeup   How to make an envelope
>
> How to do exercises   How to set up a robot

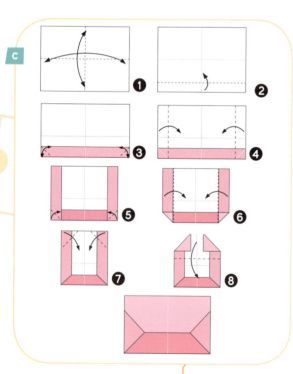

2. Look at texts 1 and 2 in activities 3 and 4. Then check the appropriate options.

a. The texts are...
- [ ] divided into topics.
- [ ] continuous.

b. It is possible to say that the texts are related to...
- [ ] doing offline research.
- [ ] doing research (online and offline).

c. Text 1 presents...
- [ ] three steps.
- [ ] five steps.

d. Text 2 presents...
- [ ] five steps.
- [ ] six steps.

Reading

3. Read text 1 and number the steps according to the instruction each one relates to.

Text 1

5 WAYS to Make Online Research Easier

Going online to do research when you're writing papers and doing projects is a no-brainer. Here are five ways to make researching online as easy and effective as possible:

1. Start at school. Ask your teachers or the librarian which resources they recommend for your project.

2. Sort fact from fiction. Make a list of the kinds of sites that are best for your topic. Is the website reliable and up to date? Check to see if the author is identified and if the sources are cited.

3. Search smart. Use more specific terms when doing your research. The results will be better this way.

4. Stay focused. Stay focused on your research by logging off of social media and email (and turn off your phone!).

5. Cite right. When you research online, it can be easy to copy and paste text, then forget to cite the source. Even accidental plagiarism can have serious consequences — so don't take a chance.

Adapted from <http://kidshealth.org/en/teens/online-research.html>. Accessed on February 26, 2019.

a. [ ] Concentrate on your research by disconnecting from social media and switching off your phone.
b. [ ] Talk to your teacher or the librarian.
c. [ ] Cite the source where you found the information.
d. [ ] Check if the website is reliable and if it cites its sources.
e. [ ] Be clear and go straight to the point.

L1

4 Now read text 2 and put the steps in the appropriate order according to it.

Text 2

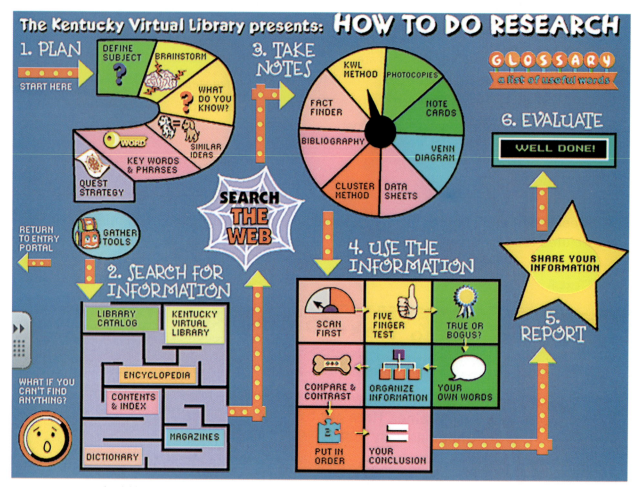

Available at <https://www.libfocus.com/2012/07/how-to-do-research-for-kids.html>. Accessed on February 26, 2019.

a ☐ Do some research in libraries, encyclopedias, dictionaries and magazines.
b ☐ Organize the information, compare and contrast it to check if it is true.
c ☐ Evaluate your research.
d ☐ Use previous knowledge and think of key words and phrases.
e ☐ Take notes.
f ☐ Share the information you found.

Post-reading

5 Based on the texts, check if the statements are *T* (true) or *F* (false).

a ☐ Text 1 does not have pictures to illustrate and explain the steps.
b ☐ Text 2 has a detailed explanation for each step.
c ☐ Texts 1 and 2 are used to give instructions.

L2

Toolbox Present simple (review)

1 Look at the pictures. Which activities are represented in them?

- [ ] chat
- [ ] listen to music
- [ ] listen to podcasts
- [ ] read books
- [ ] read the news
- [ ] research
- [ ] study
- [ ] talk to friends
- [ ] use social media
- [ ] watch videos

2 How often do you do the activities from activity 1? Take a look at the chart and talk about your habits. Work in pairs.

always	usually	normally	often/ frequently	sometimes	occasionally	seldom	rarely	never
100%	90%	80%	70%	50%	30%	10%	5%	0%

Useful language

I **usually** go online in the afternoon.
My brother **occasionally** reads books on his tablet.
We **never** post on social media when we're at school.

3 Read the transcripts of the video about things that Tristan and Lauren do online. Then check the appropriate sentences.

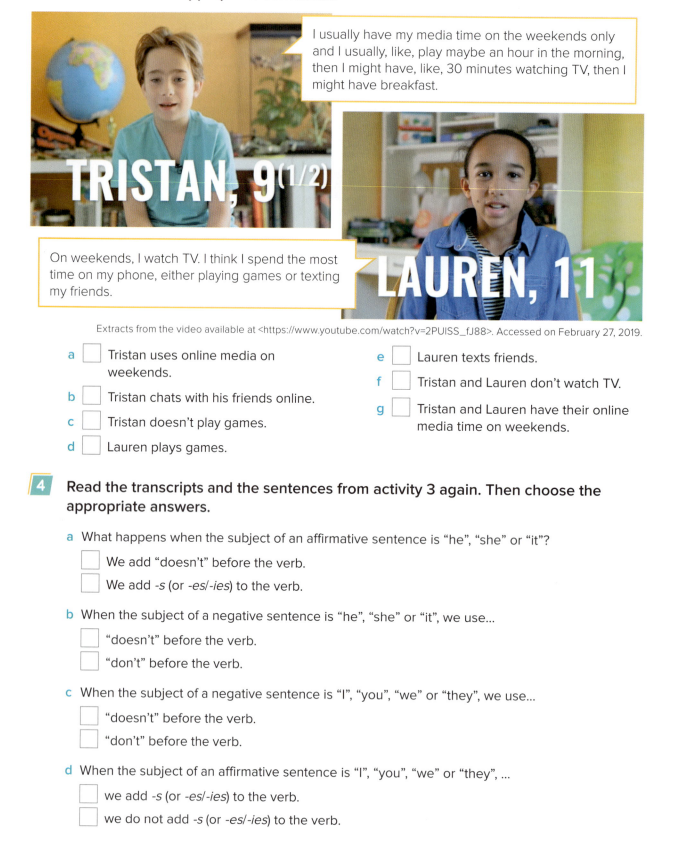

I usually have my media time on the weekends only and I usually, like, play maybe an hour in the morning, then I might have, like, 30 minutes watching TV, then I might have breakfast.

TRISTAN, 9 (1/2)

On weekends, I watch TV. I think I spend the most time on my phone, either playing games or texting my friends.

LAUREN, 11

Extracts from the video available at <https://www.youtube.com/watch?v=2PUISS_fJ88>. Accessed on February 27, 2019.

a ☐ Tristan uses online media on weekends.
b ☐ Tristan chats with his friends online.
c ☐ Tristan doesn't play games.
d ☐ Lauren plays games.
e ☐ Lauren texts friends.
f ☐ Tristan and Lauren don't watch TV.
g ☐ Tristan and Lauren have their online media time on weekends.

4 Read the transcripts and the sentences from activity 3 again. Then choose the appropriate answers.

a What happens when the subject of an affirmative sentence is "he", "she" or "it"?
   ☐ We add "doesn't" before the verb.
   ☐ We add -s (or -es/-ies) to the verb.

b When the subject of a negative sentence is "he", "she" or "it", we use…
   ☐ "doesn't" before the verb.
   ☐ "don't" before the verb.

c When the subject of a negative sentence is "I", "you", "we" or "they", we use…
   ☐ "doesn't" before the verb.
   ☐ "don't" before the verb.

d When the subject of an affirmative sentence is "I", "you", "we" or "they", …
   ☐ we add -s (or -es/-ies) to the verb.
   ☐ we do not add -s (or -es/-ies) to the verb.

5 Read a survey on what teens do online and check the appropriate option.

Teen internet activities

Do you ever...	Online Teens (n = 886)
go to websites about movies, TV shows, music groups or sports stars?	81%
get information about news and current events?	77%
send or receive instant messages (IMs)?	68%
watch videos on video-sharing sites?	57%
use an online social networking site?	55%
get information about a college or university you are thinking of attending?	55%
play computer or console games online?	49%
buy things online, such as books, clothes and music?	38%
look for health, dieting or physical fitness information?	28%
download podcasts?	19%
visit chat rooms?	18%

Adapted from *Pew Internet & American Life Project Survey of Parents and Teens*, October-November 2006.

The question "Do you ever...?" refers to...

a ☐ activities that teenagers usually do online.

b ☐ activities that teenagers used to do online in the past.

RTV

Watch: **Going viral**

6 Answer the questions according to the survey from activity 5.

a What is the most popular activity teens do online?
_____

b Do teens use social media?
_____

c Do teens use the internet more often to get information or to chat?
_____

d What are the two activities teens do that have the same popularity?
_____

7 Read the questions from activity 6 again. Then underline the appropriate option to complete each statement.

a The *wh-* word is followed by the **subject of the sentence/verb to be**.

b In an interrogative sentence, the auxiliary verb ("do"/"does") is used **before/after** the subject of the sentence.

L2

Building blocks | Gadgets

1 Match the words and expressions to the gadgets.

- [ ] cell phone/smartphone
- [ ] digital camera
- [ ] drone
- [ ] e-reader
- [ ] flash drive/memory stick
- [ ] game console with controller
- [ ] headphones
- [ ] keyboard and mouse
- [ ] laptop/notebook
- [ ] media player
- [ ] (modem) router
- [ ] portable game console
- [ ] smartwatch
- [ ] speakers
- [ ] tablet
- [ ] virtual reality headset

Language clue

A **gadget** is usually a small mechanical or electronic device with a practical use, but often considered a novelty.

Going further

When talking about technology, the words "laptop" and "notebook" are used to talk about the same device.

2 Answer the questions. Then share your answers with your classmates.
What gadget(s) do you use to...

a listen to music? _____

b read books? _____

c take pictures? _____

d play games? _____

e type? _____

Sync Listening: Internet habits

Pre-listening

1 Look at the chart. Which generation do you belong to?

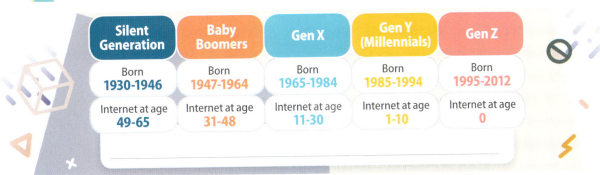

Listening

2 Listen to a boy from Singapore talking about the habits of his generation. Check the appropriate answers.

a What is his generation?
- ☐ Gen Y.
- ☐ Gen Z.

b What are examples of gadgets used by his generation?
- ☐ PCs, cell phones, gaming devices and cameras.
- ☐ PCs, smartphones, gaming devices, tablets and MP3 players.

c What is their main characteristic?
- ☐ They naturally multitask.
- ☐ They don't know how to multitask.

d What are the activities that his generation does at the same time?
- ☐ They text and read, but cannot watch and walk at the same time.
- ☐ They text, read, watch and walk at the same time.

3 Listen to another excerpt of the audio and write *T* (true) or *F* (false).
People from Gen Z…

a ☐ send letters via mail.
b ☐ spend 20% of their time on social media.
c ☐ spend most of their time outdoors.
d ☐ stay at home.

Post-listening

4 Do you agree with the ideas presented in the audio? Check the statements you agree with.

a ☐ Generation Z is good at multitasking.
b ☐ Generation Z shows their feelings and shares them with the world.
c ☐ Generation Z prefers staying at home to playing outside and being physically active.

L3

Sync Speaking: Presentation of a survey

Pre-speaking

1 🎧 4 Listen to the answers to a survey on the use of the internet in Canada and match the people to the way they use the internet.

a Interviewee 1   b Interviewee 2   c Interviewee 3

☐ news and general information
☐ entertainment, communication and research
☐ connection with friends

2 Interview some people in your school and find the following information.

a What generation do they belong to? _____

b How many of them use the internet…

   I   to talk to friends and family? _____

   II to work? _____

   III to study/do research? _____

   IV to have fun (entertainment)? _____

Speaking

3 Now present your survey results to your classmates.

> **Useful language**
> Ana uses the internet for entertainment. She is from Generation Z.
> Jorge doesn't use the internet. He is a Baby Boomer.
> Most people in my survey use the internet to connect with friends.

Post-speaking

4 Create a graphic that represents the results of your survey.

Studio Tutorial

> **What:** a tutorial
> **To whom:** classmates and the community
> **Media:** paper; digital
> **Objective:** create a written tutorial

1. Think of some topics you are good at or some problem you know how to solve.
2. Define the format of your tutorial.
3. Write a step-by-step guide.
4. If necessary, add some notes to explain the steps.
5. Share your tutorial with a partner and ask for feedback. Give him/her some feedback too.
6. Revise your work.
7. Share your tutorial with your classmates.
8. Publish your work on the **Students for PEACE Social Media** <www.studentsforpeace.com.br>, using the tag **mytutorial** or others chosen by the students.

2 Expression

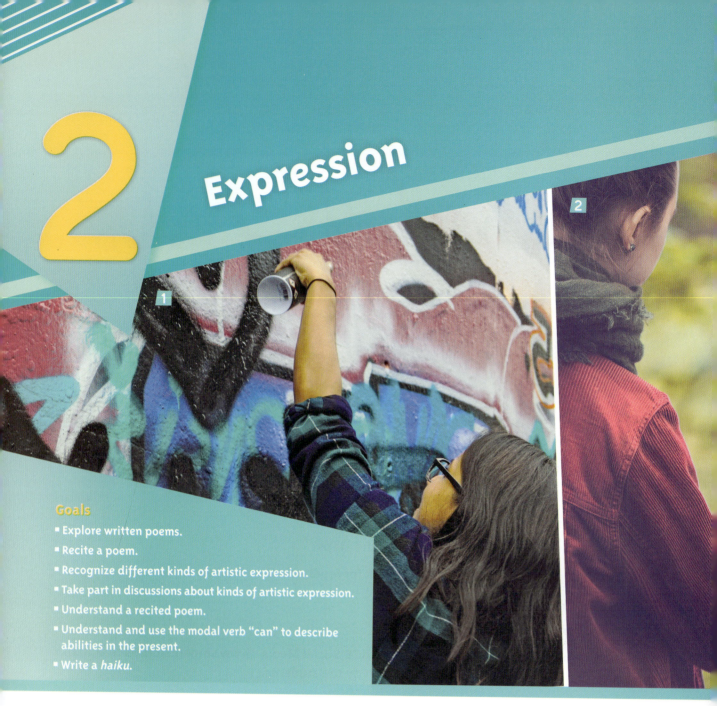

Goals
- Explore written poems.
- Recite a poem.
- Recognize different kinds of artistic expression.
- Take part in discussions about kinds of artistic expression.
- Understand a recited poem.
- Understand and use the modal verb "can" to describe abilities in the present.
- Write a *haiku*.

Spark

1 Look at the pictures and do the activities.

a What kind of expression does each picture represent? Write *1* to *4* according to the number of the pictures.

☐ graffiti ☐ music ☐ painting ☐ poetry

b Match the artistic expressions represented in the pictures to the appropriate materials.

☐ canvas ☐ pen
☐ musical instruments ☐ spray paint

c Which kinds of artistic expression have you ever used to express yourself? Check them.

- [ ] dance
- [ ] graffiti
- [ ] music
- [ ] painting
- [ ] photography
- [ ] poetry
- [ ] sculpture
- [ ] theater

2 Take a look at the artistic expressions mentioned in activity 1. Do you know other kinds of expression? Write them.

_____
_____
_____

L1

Pre-reading

1 In your opinion, what could be the subject of a poem?
- a ☐ human behavior
- b ☐ humor
- c ☐ love
- d ☐ nations and people
- e ☐ nature
- f ☐ war

2 Take a look at the poems in activity 3 and pay attention to their keywords. Can you guess each poem's theme?

_____
_____

Reading

3 Now read the poems. Then write *T* (true) or *F* (false).

Text 1

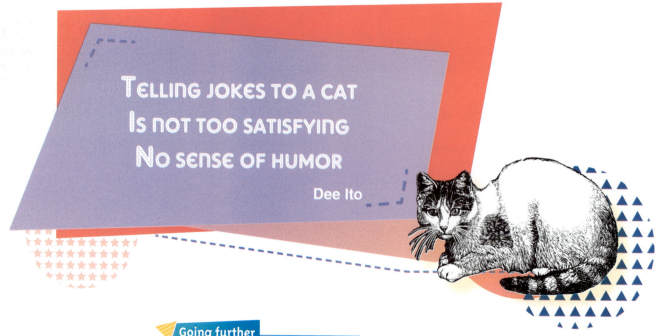

TELLING JOKES TO A CAT
IS NOT TOO SATISFYING
NO SENSE OF HUMOR

Dee Ito

Going further

Haiku is a traditional form of Japanese poetry. It usually talks about a particular moment.

Text 2

CAN'T YOU SEE

Can't you see
I just want to have a friend
Can't you see
I need the same connections in the end

Can't you see
I want a good job
Can't you see
I need to have stability and [...] be part of the general mob

Can't you see
I want to be independent on my own
Can't you see
I want to be able to have my own home

Can't you see
I want the same things as everyone else
Can't you see
I want to be appreciated for myself

Scott Lentine

a ☐ Texts 1 and 2 have the same structure and style.

b ☐ Text 1 describes the poet's frustration when telling something funny to a cat.

c ☐ In text 2, the poet wishes to be treated as someone different and unique.

d ☐ In text 2, the poet has common desires.

Going further

Scott Lentine is an American poet with high-functioning autism (Asperger's). He works to convince politicians to pass laws which help improve the lives of people with developmental disabilities.

4 According to text 2, the poet wants...

a ☐ to have a friend.
b ☐ to travel and get to know new cultures.
c ☐ a good job.
d ☐ to be part of a group and feel like everybody else.

5 Which words rhyme in text 2?

_____

_____

L1

6 Read the *haikus* and answer the questions.

> This photo album —
> Bookworms are also nourished
> With old memories
>
> Edson Iura

> ONLY THE BRAVE ARE HAPPY
>
> Without asking, the wind
> Sheds the flowers on the ground...
> I never dared
>
> Afrânio Peixoto

a Do these *haikus* have rhymes?
_____

b Do these *haikus* have the same number of lines?
_____

c Which *haiku* has a title? What is the title?
_____

Post-reading

7 What are the differences between a *haiku* and a poem? Write *poems* or *haikus*.

a _____ have only 3 lines.

b _____ usually have rhymes.

c _____ may have many lines.

d _____ traditionally talk about a particular moment.

8 In your opinion, what kind of attitudes could make the author of the poem "Can't you see" feel happy and respected?

a ☐ Being gentle with him.

b ☐ Making fun of him.

c ☐ Talking to him.

d ☐ Offering him a good job.

e ☐ Treating him like a different person.

Toolbox "Can"/"Can't"

1 Look at the comic strips in activities 2 and 3. What are their themes?

a ☐ poetry and graffiti b ☐ poetry and painting c ☐ sculpture and painting

2 Read the comic strip and check if the statements are *T* (true) or *F* (false).

a ☐ The boy says he can notice that his grandfather is writing poems.

b ☐ According to the sentence "I can tell 'cause you're wearing your cowboy hat.", the boy discovered the theme of his grandfather's poem because of the shirt he is wearing.

c ☐ According to the suggestion that the boy gives his grandfather, it is possible to say that he didn't like his grandfather's poem very much.

d ☐ The boy thinks his grandfather's cowboy hat would harmonize with cowboy boots.

3 Read this comic strip and check the appropriate options.

a The girl helps the kid by…
  ☐ finding his red paint.
  ☐ lending him some red paint.

b It is possible to say that the kid…
  ☐ uses red paint frequently.
  ☐ does not use a lot of red paint.

c After having her red paint back, the girl is…
  ☐ not sad, because she doesn't like red.
  ☐ sad, because she doesn't have any more red paint to use.

d After reading the whole comic strip, it is possible to say that the kid needs the girl's paint because he…
  ☐ used all his red paint.
  ☐ lost his red paint somewhere.

L2

4 Now read another comic strip. Then check the appropriate options.

a It is possible to say that the client's order is…
- [ ] unexpected.
- [ ] absurd.

b What makes the comic strip funny is that the client…
- [ ] does not like the artist's cakes.
- [ ] wants a simple cake.

5 Read the sentences and underline the appropriate options.

> "I can tell 'cause you're wearing your cowboy hat."

> "I can't find my red paint!"

> "Can you make it look like a cake?"

a In affirmative sentences, we use the **subject/modal verb "can"** followed by the **subject/modal verb "can"** + verb without "to".

b In negative sentences, we use the **subject/modal verb "can't"** followed by the **subject/modal verb "can't"** + verb without "to".

c In interrogative sentences, we use the **subject/modal verb "can"** followed by the **subject/modal verb "can"** + verb without "to".

RTV

Watch:
Polysemy

Useful language

"Can" is used to make informal requests:
Can you read the text, please?
"Can" is also used to ask for permission:
Can I borrow your pencil, please?

Language clue

The word "can" has different meanings, that depend on the context. It can be:
- the modal verb used to talk about abilities;
- a metal container.

L2

Building blocks Expressions

1 Look at the pictures. Can you do these activities? Use the chart to classify them according to your abilities.

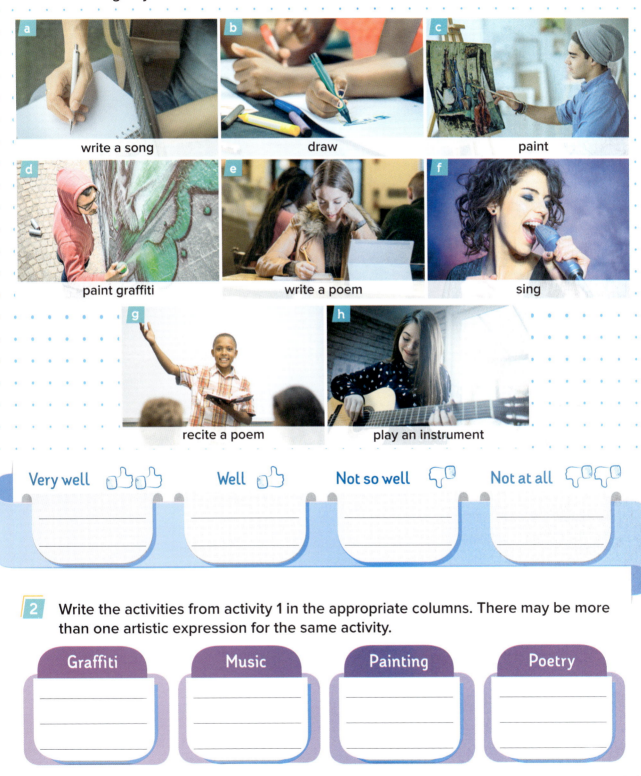

a. write a song
b. draw
c. paint
d. paint graffiti
e. write a poem
f. sing
g. recite a poem
h. play an instrument

Very well 👍👍 Well 👍 Not so well 👎 Not at all 👎👎

2 Write the activities from activity 1 in the appropriate columns. There may be more than one artistic expression for the same activity.

Graffiti	Music	Painting	Poetry

3 Now talk about your abilities with a partner. Use *can* or *can't*.

L3

Sync Listening: Poetry slam

Pre-listening

1 Look at the picture and circle the appropriate options.

a Can you guess what the girl is doing?

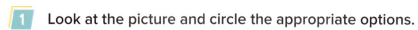

acting   playing a musical instrument   reciting a poem

b In your opinion, what is necessary for this kind of activity?

acting   clear gestures   good posture   good voice   memorization

Listening

2 🎧 5 **Listen to Pe'Tehn reciting a poem. Choose the appropriate option.**
According to the audio, it is possible to notice that the kid uses…

a ☐ an angry tone of voice.
b ☐ an encouraging tone of voice.
c ☐ a humorous tone of voice.

3 🎧 6 **Listen to the first stanza of the poem and put the lines in the appropriate order.**

a ☐ Do you know you can be
b ☐ If you try to be
c ☐ Do you know who you are
d ☐ What you want to be
e ☐ Hey, Black Child
f ☐ What you can be
g ☐ Who you really are

4 🎧 7 **Now listen to the second stanza and complete it.**

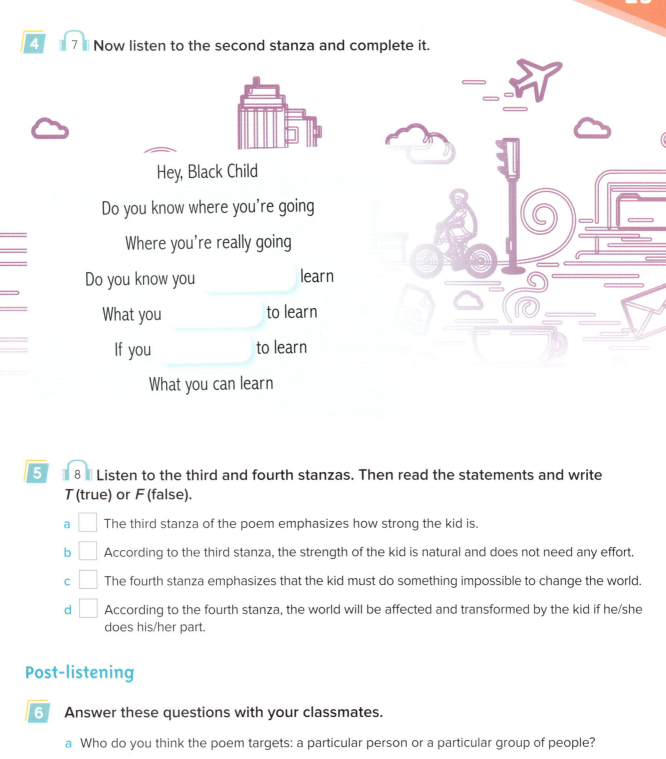

Hey, Black Child
Do you know where you're going
Where you're really going
Do you know you _____ learn
What you _____ to learn
If you _____ to learn
What you can learn

5 🎧 8 **Listen to the third and fourth stanzas. Then read the statements and write T (true) or F (false).**

a ☐ The third stanza of the poem emphasizes how strong the kid is.

b ☐ According to the third stanza, the strength of the kid is natural and does not need any effort.

c ☐ The fourth stanza emphasizes that the kid must do something impossible to change the world.

d ☐ According to the fourth stanza, the world will be affected and transformed by the kid if he/she does his/her part.

Post-listening

6 **Answer these questions with your classmates.**

a Who do you think the poem targets: a particular person or a particular group of people?

_____

b In your opinion, can other people benefit from the poem's message?

_____

Going further

The poem **"Hey, Black Child"** was written by Useni Eugene Perkins, an American poet, playwright and youth worker.

L3

Sync Speaking: *Poetry soirée*

Pre-speaking

1 In your opinion, what should an interesting poem have?

- a ☐ adventure
- b ☐ drama
- c ☐ history
- d ☐ humor
- e ☐ nature
- f ☐ philosophy
- g ☐ romance
- h ☐ social criticism

Speaking

2 You are going to recite a poem. Work in small groups and follow the instructions.

a Tell your classmates the poem you have chosen.

b Discuss the theme of each poem in your group: do you agree with the poems' ideas?

c Practice your recitation. Share it with your group.

d Listen to your classmates' recitation and give them some feedback.

e Try to memorize your poem.

f Recite your poem to your classmates.

Useful language
Bravo!
Congratulations!
Great job!
Well done!

Post-speaking

3 Answer these questions with your classmates.

a In your opinion, is reading a poem different from reciting a poem?

_____
_____

b Think about your classmates' poems. Which ones did you like the most?

_____
_____

Studio *Haiku*

> **What:** a *haiku*
> **To whom:** other students; school community; the internet
> **Media:** paper; digital
> **Objective:** express a feeling or an idea

1. Make a list of the themes you would like to explore. Then choose one.
2. Think of some keywords related to the topic you've chosen.
3. Write your *haiku*.
4. Share your poem with a partner and read his/her *haiku* too. Give feedback to each other.
5. Revise and illustrate your *haiku*.
6. Show your *haiku* to your classmates.
7. Read and illustrate a classmate's *haiku*.
8. Compare each author's illustration to a reader's illustration.
9. Publish your work on the **Students for PEACE Social Media** <www.studentsforpeace.com.br>, using the tag **haiku** or others chosen by the students.

Peace talk

Chapters 1 and 2
Be yourself

1 Read the title of this text. What do you think the subject is?
_____

Children's COMMISSIONER
ABOUT US   OUR WORK   LATEST NEWS   PUBLICATIONS

Life in Likes

1 Children become increasingly anxious about their online image and "keeping up appearances" as they get older. 2 This can be made worse when they start to follow celebrities and others outside close family and friends. 3 Their use of platforms on the internet can also undermine children's view of themselves by making them feel inferior to the people they follow.

> 4 Harry, 11, Year 6: "When you get 50 likes, it makes you feel good cos you know people think you look good in that photo."
>
> 5 Aaron, 11, Year 7: "If I got 150 likes, I'd be like 'that's pretty cool', it means they like you."
>
> 6 Aimee, 11, Year 7: "You might compare yourself cos you're not very pretty compared to them."
>
> 7 Annie, 11, Year 7: "I just edit my photos to make sure I look nice."
>
> 8 Harry, 11, Year 6: "If you don't have designer and expensive things, people will make fun of you."

Adapted from <https://www.childrenscommissioner.gov.uk/2018/01/04/children-unprepared-for-social-media-cliff-edge-as-they-start-secondary-school-childrens-commissioner-for-england-warns-in-new-report/>. Accessed on May 31, 2019.

2 Read the text in activity 1 and number these statements 1-8 accordingly.

a ☐ Um pré-adolescente associa a quantidade de *likes* com a aceitação de sua aparência na foto.

b ☐ Uma pré-adolescente menciona a importância de editar suas fotos para melhorar sua aparência.

c ☐ Afirma-se que, à medida que as crianças crescem, aumenta a ansiedade em relação à sua imagem na internet.

d ☐ Um pré-adolescente acredita que precisa ter coisas caras para não sofrer deboches.

e ☐ Afirma-se que o uso de redes sociais pode fazer as crianças se sentirem insatisfeitas com sua própria imagem.

f ☐ Afirma-se que seguir, em redes sociais, pessoas famosas e que não façam parte da família da criança aumenta a ansiedade em relação à sua própria imagem.

g ☐ Um pré-adolescente associa a quantidade de *likes* que recebe à quantidade de pessoas que gostam dele.

h ☐ Uma pré-adolescente diz que a comparação com outras pessoas a faz se sentir menos bonita.

3 Discuss these questions with your classmates.

a Que tipo de problema relacionado ao uso de plataformas *online* o texto da atividade 1 apresenta?

b De que outras maneiras é possível reagir positivamente à postagem da foto de um/a amigo/a em uma rede social sem focar na aparência?

c As redes sociais possibilitam que as pessoas se expressem de vários modos e com praticidade. Em sua opinião, como é possível usar esse recurso de forma que proporcione satisfação real em vez de ansiedade, uma vez que esta pode afetar nossa autoestima?

4 Work in groups and do the activities.

a Leiam a frase abaixo. É uma citação atribuída ao escritor irlandês Oscar Wilde. Considerando tudo o que foi discutido nesta seção, o que essa frase quer dizer?

_____

_____

b Façam um cartaz inspirador. Sigam as instruções.

I Busquem outras frases em inglês que sirvam de inspiração para as pessoas serem o que são em vez de tentar ser aquilo que os/as outros/as querem ou esperam que elas sejam. É possível também criar frases inéditas.

II Escolham imagens que combinem com essas frases para compor os cartazes.

III Afixem os cartazes no mural da escola para mostrar às pessoas que ninguém precisa deixar de ser o que é para ter garantido o seu lugar em uma sociedade inclusiva.

3 Meet my culture

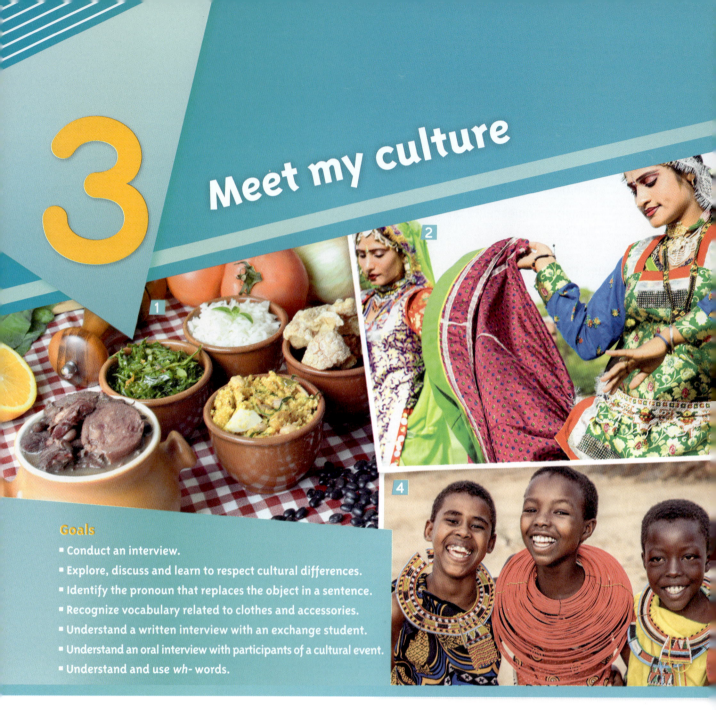

Goals
- Conduct an interview.
- Explore, discuss and learn to respect cultural differences.
- Identify the pronoun that replaces the object in a sentence.
- Recognize vocabulary related to clothes and accessories.
- Understand a written interview with an exchange student.
- Understand an oral interview with participants of a cultural event.
- Understand and use *wh-* words.

Spark

1 Match the pictures to the cultural manifestations they represent.

a ☐ art   d ☐ dance
b ☐ clothing   e ☐ greeting
c ☐ cuisine   f ☐ music

2 Which of these cultural manifestations is Brazilian?

_____

3 Do you know the other cultural manifestations represented in the pictures? Describe them.

_____
_____

4 The word "culture" can have different meanings. Check the definition that seems closer to the context of the pictures.

a ☐ Development of knowledge and the mind through study or training.

b ☐ The cultivation of plants.

c ☐ The arts, customs, behaviors and beliefs characteristic of a particular social, ethnic or age group.

d ☐ A group of microorganisms grown or taken for scientific study, medicinal use etc.

L1

Explore Interview

Pre-reading

1 Why do these people normally conduct interviews? Match the columns.

a employers

b students

c journalists

☐ To inform people about a person or topic of their interest.

☐ To research or work on a project.

☐ To get to know the people who apply for a job position.

2 What kinds of interviews are these? Match them to the pictures.

a face-to-face interview

b written interview

c press conference

d remote interview

3 Look at the interview in activity 4. Focus on the title and the information right below it. What do you think you will find in the text?

a ☐ It's an interview with a famous person.

b ☐ It's an interview with an ordinary person.

c ☐ The interviewer works at a medical institution.

d ☐ The interviewer works at an educational institution.

e ☐ The interviewee is a student who is studying in a foreign country for some period.

Reading

4 Now read the interview and match the parts of the text to the corresponding key information.

Interview with an Exchange Student

Anja Vogt, Writer
February 26, 2017

We have several exchange students here this year. They come from all over the world. I got the opportunity to sit down and talk to one of them.

Q: So, what is your name? Where do you come from originally?
A: My name is Franka Ferlemann, and I'm from Münster. It's in the northwest of Germany.

Q: What grade are you in?
A: In Germany I'm in 10th grade, and here I'm in 11th grade.

Q: How long are you staying here?
A: I came at the beginning of the second semester, and I'm staying until the end of the school year.

Q: What are some differences that you notice between Pittsburgh and Münster?
A: Let me think about that. I would say everything is bigger here. Milk cartons, at the store, are giant! People are friendlier here. They're more open. And the school is different: the whole school system and how it works.

Q: What are some things that you like or dislike about Pittsburgh or the U.S.?
A: Well, Pittsburgh is really beautiful, the outdoor landscape is very pretty. What I don't like is that the weather changes so much in this season. But, overall, I'm pretty happy here!

Q: How do you feel speaking English? You seem to speak very well.
A: Thank you! I mean, sometimes I can understand, but sometimes people talk very fast. And kids will also use a lot of slang, which is hard to know.

Q: Why did you decide to come here?
A: I wanted to learn more English and get to know a new culture. You always see American high schools in movies, and I wanted to see if it was really like that.

Q: Well, thanks for talking with me!
A: Yes, you're welcome!

Adapted from <https://www.obamaeagle.org/all-posts/news/2017/02/26/interview-with-an-exchange-student/>.
Accessed on March 22, 2019.

a The student's grade at school.

b Comparisons between the city where she is from and the city where she studies now.

c What she likes and doesn't like about the city or country where she is studying now.

d The student's difficulties related to the language she is learning.

e Reasons why she decided to study in a foreign country.

f How long she intends to study at the foreign country.

g The student's name and nationality.

L1

5 Answer these questions.

a What sentence from the text tells us that there are students of many different nationalities in Pittsburgh?

_____

b Franka has some difficulties in Pittsburgh, but they are not a real problem for her. Which sentence proves that?

_____

6 Find words/expressions from the interview that you can use to label the following items.

Post-reading

7 Answer these questions with your classmates.

a Who would you like to interview? Would you like to be interviewed?

_____

b Would you like to have the experience of being an exchange student? Check the reasons.

- ☐ different culture
- ☐ experience abroad
- ☐ foreign language
- ☐ more knowledge
- ☐ new friends
- ☐ trip

Toolbox *Wh-* words, subject and object pronouns

1 Read some of the questions taken from the interview with the German exchange student. Then answer the questions.

"WHERE DO YOU COME FROM ORIGINALLY?"

"WHAT ARE SOME DIFFERENCES THAT YOU NOTICE BETWEEN PITTSBURGH AND MÜNSTER?"

"HOW DO YOU FEEL SPEAKING ENGLISH?"

"WHY DID YOU DECIDE TO COME HERE?"

a What words are used at the beginning of the questions?
_____

b Which of those *wh-* words refers to each of the following purposes?

I  Ask for information about something: _____

II Ask about a reason: _____

III  Ask about people: **Who**

IV Ask about time: **When**

V  Ask about location: _____

VI Ask about manner: _____

2 Observe these questions and match them to the appropriate rule.

a "Where do you come from originally?"

b "What are some differences that you notice between Pittsburgh and Münster?"

☐ The question is formed with a *wh-* word + verb to be + subject.

☐ The question is formed with a *wh-* word + auxiliary verb + subject + main verb.

L2

3 Read this text, check the appropriate options and answer the questions.

You Will Develop Cultural Sensitivity

Being culturally sensitive is the key in our globalizing world. It is important to look for underlying values that may explain certain behaviors in order to practice cultural sensitivity.

A good example is when I was in Spain (especially in the south), where **they** take a 2-3 hour *siesta* and lunch in the middle of their workday. Many people view this cultural norm as the people just being lazy, when it really has a lot more to do with the fact that, historically, Spaniards value family face time. Eating together as a family is more important to **them** than maximizing work time by scarfing a sandwich down at their desks.

Being aware of cultural values and norms is not only fascinating, but can help **us** understand international issues and conflicts. Cultural sensitivity will help you with your communication on both business and personal levels.

Adapted from <https://greenhearttravel.org/general/6-reasons-why-traveling-abroad-is-important-for-young-people>. Accessed on March 22, 2019.

a Who does the word "they" refer to in the second paragraph?
☐ Culturally sensitive people.   ☐ People from the south of Spain.

b Who does the word "them" refer to in the second paragraph?
☐ Spaniards.   ☐ People who are lazy.

c Who does the word "us" in the third paragraph refer to?
☐ You, the reader.   ☐ We, people in general.

d Which of these words ("they", "them", "us") functions as a subject pronoun (the one that performs the action)? _____

e Which of them function as an object pronoun (the one that receives the action or follows a preposition)? _____

f Based on the examples provided in the text, complete the chart with the missing pronouns.

Subject pronouns	Object pronouns
I	me
you	you
he	him
she	her
it	it
we	
you	you

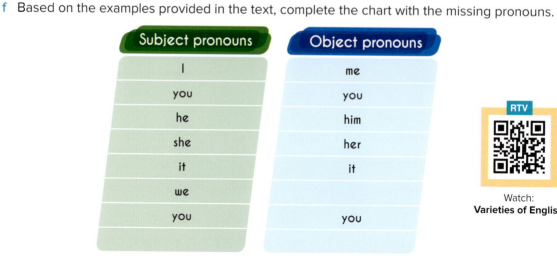

Watch:
Varieties of English

Building blocks: Clothes and accessories

1 Which items of clothing and accessories can you name? Match the pictures to the words.

a	☐ cap	c	☐ jeans	e	☐ shirt	g	☐ sneakers	i	☐ T-shirt
b	☐ dress	d	☐ pants	f	☐ skirt	h	☐ tank top	j	☐ vest

2 What kinds of clothes and accessories do you usually wear in each of these situations? Write sentences using the following ideas.

I usually wear... to go to school.

I prefer to wear... to go to the mall with my family.

a

to go to school

_____
_____

b

to go to the mall

_____
_____

c

to go to a party

_____
_____

d

to stay at home

_____
_____

L2

3 Who are these people? Read the descriptions and write their names according to what they are wearing.

a Daniel is wearing pants and a hoodie. He is also wearing sneakers.
b Thomas is wearing a shirt and a jacket. He is wearing bracelets too.
c Jessica is wearing sunglasses, shorts and a tank top.
d Chloe is wearing sneakers, a skirt and a necklace.

4 Write *T* (true) or *F* (false) according to your opinion. Then discuss your answers with a partner.

a ☐ All teenagers like the same kind of clothes.
b ☐ Teens don't care about the way they dress.
c ☐ Culture interferes in the way people dress.
d ☐ Most teenagers use their clothing style as a means of expression to the world.
e ☐ People are influenced in their choice of clothing by culture, celebrities and their own style and personality.
f ☐ When traveling abroad, it is important to know how people from that country are used to dressing.
g ☐ Kids and teenagers should wear a uniform at school.

L3

Sync Listening: An interview at an event

Pre-listening

1 Look at the picture and read the caption. Make predictions by answering the questions.

Wacipi: the annual celebration of the Shakopee Mdewakanton Sioux Community

a What type of event is this?

☐ An Olympic opening ceremony.
☐ A cultural event about indigenous peoples/communities.

b What kinds of sounds do you expect to hear in an event like this?

☐ animal sounds   ☐ singing
☐ applause   ☐ people talking
☐ musical instruments

Listening

2 🎧 9 Listen to three people talking about the event and check if your predictions were correct.

3 🎧 9 Listen again and number the topics in the order they are mentioned.

FLAGS AND EAGLE STAFFS

THE BEAT OF THE DRUM

CELEBRATION OF LIFE

Post-listening

4 Use the phrases from activity 3 to complete this summary of the interview.

The participants of the Wacipi (also known as "Powwow") say that the event is a _____ and it's where they meet friends and relatives. The grand entry is symbolic because the _____ represent nations. The heart of the celebration is _____ because it's the moment when people come together.

43

L3

Sync Speaking: Interviewing someone

Pre-speaking

1 Do the following activities.

a Circle the words from the box that would be relevant to interview someone from another culture.

> architecture   art   beliefs   celebrations   clothes   customs   education
> food   greetings   history   language   music   sports   technology

b Take a look at the picture. What do you think these people could tell about their culture?

2 Follow the instructions to get ready to interview someone.

a Think of someone who is from another culture.

b Write questions to him/her according to some of the categories mentioned in activity 1.

c Share your questions with a partner and give feedback to each other.

Useful language
How important is education/tradition/mealtime in your culture?
What are some of the customs in your culture?
What important dates are celebrated? What is the history behind them?
What is considered (dis)respectful in your culture?

Speaking

3 Interview the person you have chosen. You can take notes of his/her answers or record them.

Post-speaking

4 Read the statements and check the ones you agree with.

a ☐ It is possible to understand people's behaviors and reactions when we know more about their culture.

b ☐ Some people are prejudiced regarding some aspects of culture that they don't know much about.

c ☐ You can always learn from different people and cultures.

Studio | Interview transcript

What: an interview transcript
To whom: classmates
Media: paper; digital
Objective: transcribe an oral interview

1. What is the structure of an interview? Read the interview presented in the "Explore" section again and take notes.
2. Transcribe the interview you conducted in the "Sync – Speaking" section.
3. What information is important for the readers to know before reading this interview? Write a brief introduction for it.
4. Share your text with a partner and ask for feedback. Give him/her some feedback too.
5. Revise your text.
6. Choose three interviews to read. Share them with your group and discuss the cultures mentioned in them.
7. Gather all the interviews and organize a book.
8. Publish your work on the **Students for PEACE Social Media** <www.studentsforpeace.com.br>, using the tag **interview** or others chosen by the students.

4 Food and nutrition

Goals
- Distinguish between countable and uncountable nouns.
- Learn vocabulary related to food.
- Read and create a cooking recipe.
- Read and understand a text with nutritional information.
- Understand an audio with suggestions for a healthy diet.
- Understand and use adverbs of frequency to talk about eating habits.
- Understand and use the imperative in recipe instructions.

Spark

1 Look at the pictures. What meals do they show?

a Breakfast: _____   c Dinner: _____

b Lunch: _____   d Snack: _____

2 In which pictures can you see the following items?

a ☐ apple   e ☐ cheese
b ☐ banana   f ☐ chicken fillet
c ☐ beans   g ☐ egg
d ☐ bread

h ☐ fish
i ☐ granola
j ☐ olive oil
k ☐ orange juice
l ☐ rice
m ☐ salad

3 Which of the food items mentioned in activity 2 are part of your diet?

L1

Explore Recipe

Pre-reading

1 Look at texts 1 and 2 in activities 2 and 4. Then check the appropriate options.

a What is the purpose of text 1?

☐ To teach the reader how to cook.
☐ To inform the reader about healthy eating habits.

b What is the purpose of text 2?

☐ To tell about Nargisse's eating habits.
☐ To teach the reader how to cook a typical Moroccan dish.

Reading

2 Read text 1 and write if the statements are *T* (true) or *F* (false).

Text 1

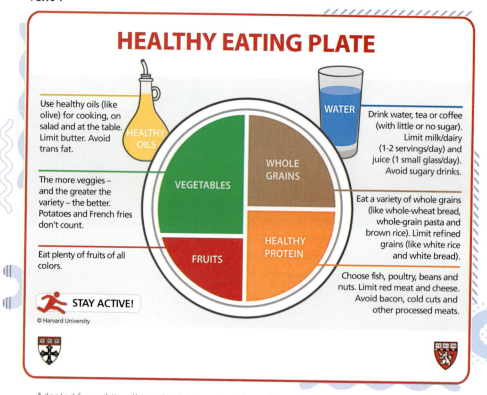

Adapted from <https://www.hsph.harvard.edu/news/magazine/centennial-food-guides-history/>.
Accessed on March 31, 2019.

☐ The text divides food items into seven categories.
☐ The text only mentions information about eating and drinking.
☐ The authors of the text are probably specialists from a university.
☐ The text is essentially about the importance of a colorful plate.

3 Organize the food items mentioned in **text 1** into these categories.

Use	Eat	Drink	Limit	Avoid

4 Read the text and check its main sections.

Text 2

Adapted from <http://www.mymoroccanfood.com/about>. Based on <https://newyouescapes.com/recipe/new-you-boot-camp-five-a-day-tagine/>. Accessed on March 31, 2019.

a ☐ a map of Morocco
b ☐ a list of ingredients
c ☐ instructions to prepare a Moroccan dish
d ☐ a box for comments
e ☐ information about the author

Language clue

Jacket potato: a baked potato served with the skin on.

L1

5 Find the following information in the text.

a The name of the author: _____

b The author's nationality: _____

c Why she writes her blog: _____

6 Check the food items you find in text 2.

a carrot b chicken c egg
d fish e onion f orange
g parsnip h potato i tomato

7 What category from text 1 do the food items you checked in activity 6 belong to?

_____

Post-reading

8 Answer these questions.

a Do you think you would like the *tagine*? Why?

_____

b Do you like food from other countries? Which one(s)?

_____

c Share your answers with your classmates. Are they similar to or different from yours?

_____

Listen to: **Foreign food**

L2

Toolbox: Imperative, countable and uncountable nouns

1 Look at these sentences, taken from the texts in the "Explore" section. Then choose the appropriate options.

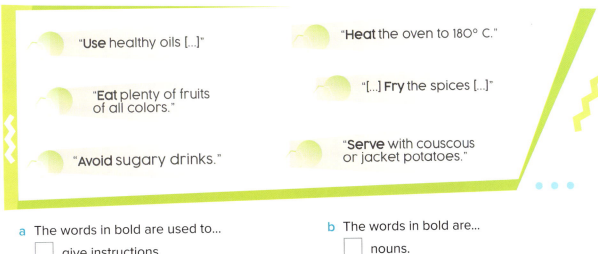

- "**Use** healthy oils [...]"
- "**Eat** plenty of fruits of all colors."
- "**Avoid** sugary drinks."
- "**Heat** the oven to 180° C."
- "[...] **Fry** the spices [...]"
- "**Serve** with couscous or jacket potatoes."

a The words in bold are used to…
- [ ] give instructions.
- [ ] make suggestions.
- [ ] make questions.
- [ ] give permission.
- [ ] give an order.
- [ ] refuse something.

b The words in bold are…
- [ ] nouns.
- [ ] verbs.
- [ ] adjectives.

c To form the imperative, we use…
- [ ] the infinitive of the verb without "to".
- [ ] the present simple with the suffix -s.

2 Complete the sentences in this guide with the imperative form of the verbs from the box.

choose (2x)   eat (2x)   get (2x)   switch

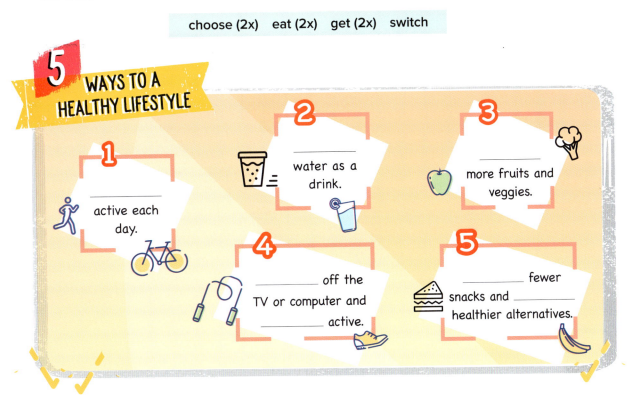

5 WAYS TO A HEALTHY LIFESTYLE

1. _____ active each day.
2. _____ water as a drink.
3. _____ more fruits and veggies.
4. _____ off the TV or computer and _____ active.
5. _____ fewer snacks and _____ healthier alternatives.

L2

3 Use the options from the box to answer the questions.

> a banana   a chicken fillet   an apple   an egg
> some milk   some orange juice   some rice   some salad

a Which food and drink items can be counted?

_____

b Which of them need measures (a cup of, a glass of, a scoop of, a bowl of)?

_____

4 Are these food and drink items countable or uncountable? Check the appropriate column.

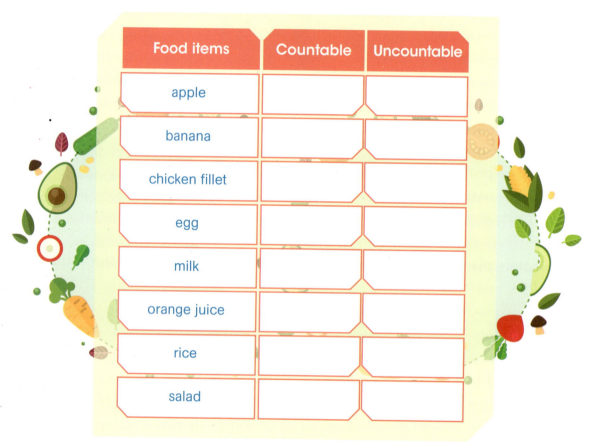

Food items	Countable	Uncountable
apple		
banana		
chicken fillet		
egg		
milk		
orange juice		
rice		
salad		

5 Which option best completes each sentence? Underline them.

a **Countable/Uncountable** nouns refer to things that can be counted using numbers.

b Things that are too small or do not have a defined shape to be counted (like liquids, gases, powders) are usually **countable/uncountable** nouns.

c **Countable/Uncountable** nouns have a singular form and a plural form (e.g.: banana/bananas).

d **Countable/Uncountable** nouns do not have a plural form (e.g.: milk, juice).

Building blocks: Adverbs of frequency and food vocabulary

1 Complete the graph and the chart according to the instructions.

a Write *0%*, *20%*, *50%*, *70%* and *100%* according to the approximate frequency for each adverb.

b Read text 1 from "Explore" again. According to its suggestions, how often should we consume the food and drink items mentioned?

Always/Usually	Sometimes	Seldom/Never

2 What about you? What are your eating habits? Complete the chart with some food and drink items according to the frequency you consume them.

Always/Usually	Sometimes	Seldom/Never

L2

3 Interview three people in your family and ask about their eating habits. Take notes and complete the chart.

Name	What they eat/drink	Frequency

> **Useful language**
> What do you eat/drink every day?
> What do you never eat/drink?
> Do you eat/drink…? How often do you eat/drink that?

4 Use the words from the box to write some of the food items used in the preparation of the dishes in the pictures.

> beans   bell pepper   bread   chickpeas   lettuce
> noodles   red meat   rice   shrimp   tofu   tomato

5 What do you usually have for lunch? And for dinner?

_____

_____

Sync Listening: *The Dietary Guidelines for the Brazilian Population*

Pre-listening

1 Answer these questions.

a What is your favorite food? _____

b Is your diet healthy? Why? _____

Listening

2 🎧 10 Listen to the first part of an audio based on the *Dietary Guidelines for the Brazilian Population*. What is the topic of this audio?

a ☐ Some food that should never be consumed.   b ☐ Balanced and healthy eating plan.

3 🎧 10 Listen to the audio again. Then complete the sentences by checking the appropriate options.

a "_____ ingredients are more balanced and have more nutrients."

☐ Natural   ☐ Fresh   ☐ Organic

b "These ingredients, in _____ quantities, add flavor to your food without harming its nutritious balance."

☐ small   ☐ moderate   ☐ minor

c "Use it only as part of a _____ based on fresh ingredients."

☐ breakfast   ☐ snack   ☐ meal

4 🎧 11 Listen to the second part of the audio and complete the sentences with the verbs mentioned in the imperative.

a "Four: _____ ultra-processed foods. They are rich in fats, sugars and additives, while low on dietary fiber."

b "Five: _____ regularly and without distraction."

c "Six: _____ food in shops offering a larger variety of fresh products, like farmer's markets."

d "Seven: _____ to develop a habit of cooking and share your cooking abilities, especially with children and youngsters."

Post-listening

5 Discuss the questions about the audio with your classmates.

a Do you agree with the guidelines? Why?

b Do you usually follow any of the suggestions given?

L3

Sync Speaking: **Presenting a recipe**

Pre-speaking

1 Look at the picture and check the appropriate options.

a What kind of program is this?

☐ A program on kitchen utensils.   ☐ A program on cooking recipes.

b What are the characteristics of the people who present this kind of program?

☐ shy   ☐ good-humored   ☐ communicative   ☐ impatient

2 Follow these instructions to plan a presentation.

a Choose a nutritious recipe to present to your classmates.

b Choose a title for your recipe and write the list of ingredients and the preparation steps.

c Share your recipe with another pair and give feedback to each other.

d Decide who is going to present each part of the recipe.

e Practice the presentation.

> **Useful language**
> Hi./Hello. We're here for one more cooking show.
> Today's recipe is…
> Attention to the ingredients. You need (a/an/some)…
> Here are the instructions for this recipe: First, (peel)… Next, (add)… Then (mix)… Finally, (serve)…
> So/Well, that's it. Hope you like it.
> Thanks and see you soon!

Speaking

3 Now host your own cooking show in class.

Post-speaking

4 Write *E* (easy) or *D* (difficult) according to your opinion about your presentation.

a ☐ Remember all the ingredients.

b ☐ Remember all the steps.

c ☐ Pronounce the name of the ingredients.

d ☐ Use the imperative appropriately.

e ☐ Speak naturally.

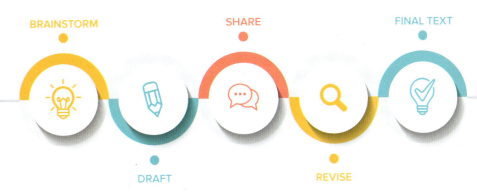

What: a recipe
To whom: other students, readers from all over the world
Media: paper; digital
Objective: share a special recipe with other people

1. Does your family have a special dish? Do you have a favorite one? Choose a recipe to share with your classmates.
2. List all the ingredients used in the recipe. In which order are they used?
3. Write your recipe.
4. Share your recipe with a partner and ask for feedback. Give him/her some feedback too.
5. Revise your text.
6. Add some pictures or drawings to your recipe.
7. Share your work with your classmates and create a Recipe Book with all the recipes presented.
8. Publish your work on the **Students for PEACE Social Media** <www.studentsforpeace.com.br>, using the tag **recipe** or others chosen by the students.

Peace talk

Chapters 3 and 4
People who eat together stay together

1 **Discuss these questions with your classmates.**

a. Você e sua família têm algum prato especial?

b. De que forma o local de origem de sua família influencia as escolhas de vocês em termos de alimentação?

c. Você gosta de pratos de outros estados ou países? Se sim, quais? É preciso viajar até esses locais para poder experimentar sua gastronomia? Justifique.

d. Você se considera uma pessoa que gosta de experimentar diferentes culinárias? Responda com exemplos.

e. Na sua opinião, a culinária pode unir as pessoas? Se sim, de que maneira?

2 **How can food help promote a Culture of Peace? Talk to a partner.**

3 **Read the interview and answer the questions.**

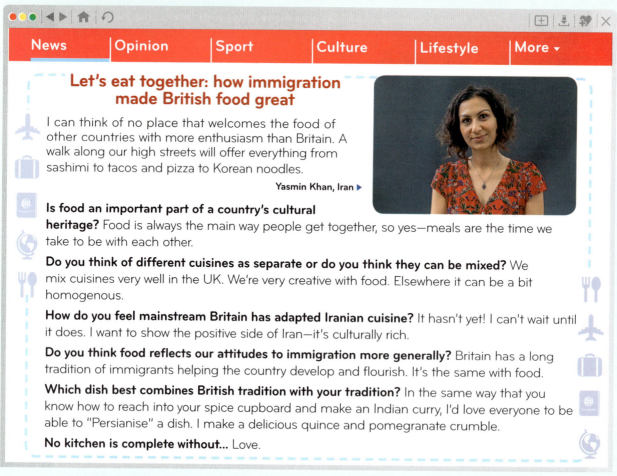

News | Opinion | Sport | Culture | Lifestyle | More

Let's eat together: how immigration made British food great

I can think of no place that welcomes the food of other countries with more enthusiasm than Britain. A walk along our high streets will offer everything from sashimi to tacos and pizza to Korean noodles.

Yasmin Khan, Iran ▶

Is food an important part of a country's cultural heritage? Food is always the main way people get together, so yes—meals are the time we take to be with each other.

Do you think of different cuisines as separate or do you think they can be mixed? We mix cuisines very well in the UK. We're very creative with food. Elsewhere it can be a bit homogenous.

How do you feel mainstream Britain has adapted Iranian cuisine? It hasn't yet! I can't wait until it does. I want to show the positive side of Iran—it's culturally rich.

Do you think food reflects our attitudes to immigration more generally? Britain has a long tradition of immigrants helping the country develop and flourish. It's the same with food.

Which dish best combines British tradition with your tradition? In the same way that you know how to reach into your spice cupboard and make an Indian curry, I'd love everyone to be able to "Persianise" a dish. I make a delicious quince and pomegranate crumble.

No kitchen is complete without... Love.

Adapted from <https://www.theguardian.com/global/2015/may/24/lets-eat-together-cooking-immigration-britain-food>.
Accessed on May 31, 2019.

a Que parte do texto indica que, no mundo, são construídas imagens negativas em relação a um país, uma região, uma cultura etc.?

b Sobre o assunto abordado no item "a", de que outras maneiras, além da que o texto propõe, podemos desconstruir estereótipos relacionados a lugares, povos e culturas?

c Que parte do texto sugere que culturas diferentes podem conviver em harmonia?

d Que partes do texto indicam que a comida tem o poder de unir as pessoas?

4 Which other parts of the text can you relate to the Culture of Peace?

5 Work with your classmates. Follow the instructions to create a Cultural Food Festival.

a Verifiquem se há, na sua turma e na escola, pessoas que são ou cujas famílias são de outras regiões do Brasil ou do mundo. Peçam a elas que comentem sobre a culinária de sua região. Façam perguntas nos moldes das que foram feitas a Yasmin Khan.

b Verifiquem o interesse dessas pessoas em apresentar algo sobre a culinária de sua região de origem num evento cultural. Se concordarem, peçam-lhes que preparem um prato típico e tragam para o evento, numa data estipulada por sua turma.

c Anotem quais pratos serão apresentados no Cultural Food Festival e pesquisem sobre suas respectivas regiões. Elaborem pôsteres para compartilhar essas informações culturais com o público. Considerem a possibilidade de mostrar mapas, fotos, gráficos etc.

d Calculem quantas pessoas participarão do festival e se as quantidades de comida serão suficientes para que todos/as provem um pouco de cada culinária contemplada.

e Se for possível, considerem também incluir no evento apresentações musicais ou de dança típicas da região de origem das pessoas. A exibição de vídeos também pode servir a esse propósito.

f Certifiquem-se de reservar um momento durante o evento para abordar com o público o conceito de Cultura de Paz, sensibilizando as pessoas sobre o papel da culinária na promoção da paz e da união entre os povos.

5 Entertainment

Goals
- Discuss different forms of entertainment.
- Explore and create a timeline.
- Identify the use of the prepositions of time "in", "on" and "at".
- Recognize the different pronunciations of regular verbs in the past (-ed).
- Understand an audio in which people react to some technology from the past.
- Use the past simple to understand and create oral and written texts.

Spark

1 Match the pictures to their descriptions.

☐ People watching a movie.   ☐ A boy listening to music.
☐ People playing a video game.   ☐ People watching a play.

2 What do these activities have in common?

a ☐ They are outdoor activities.
b ☐ They are technological activities.
c ☐ They are entertainment activities.

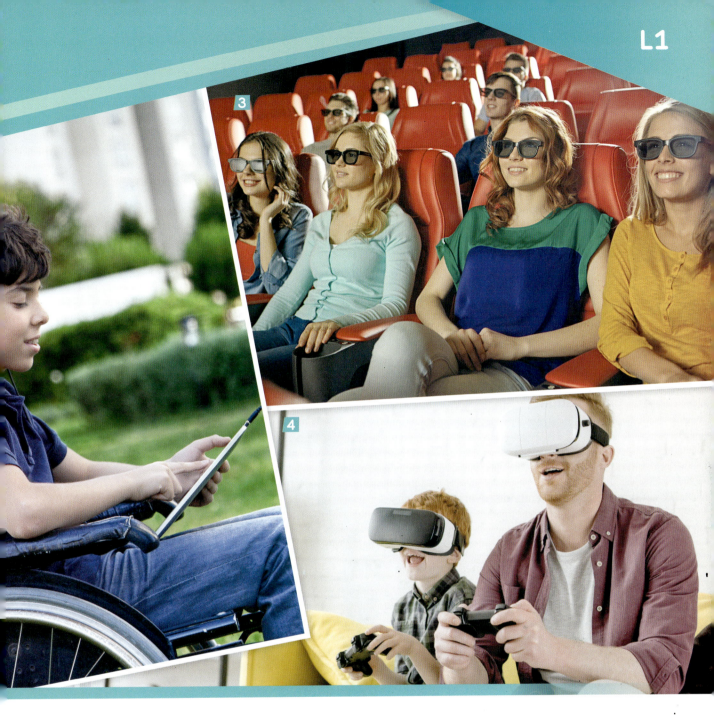

3 Do you like doing any of these activities? Which one(s)?

_____

4 How do you do these activities? Alone, with your family or with your friends?

_____

5 What has changed in the last decades? Check the appropriate option.

a ☐ Some of these forms of entertainment have disappeared.

b ☐ People stopped going to the theater and to the movies.

c ☐ The same activities can be done in a different way.

L1

Explore Timeline

Pre-reading

1 Take a look at the text in activity 2. Then check the appropriate options.

a Which of these elements does the text have?

☐ chronological order ☐ long texts ☐ pictures ☐ subtitles

b What is the purpose of this kind of text?

☐ To convince people of something. ☐ To present some events about a certain topic.

Reading

2 Read the text and discuss with your classmates. What is the most interesting information?

TIMELINE OF TELEVISION
Important moments in TV history

1775
Count Alessandro Volta discovered electricity made from friction.

1876
American inventor George Carey first described a full recording and reproducing camera system that was based on selenium.

1900
The word "television" was coined during the first International Congress of Electricity, at the World's Fair in Paris, by Russian scientist Constantin Perskyi.

1923
Russian Vladimir Zworykin patented his TV camera tube system, which would later become the cornerstone of future TV technology.

1927
The Bell Telephone Company performed the first transfer of video image between Washington D.C. and New York City. In the same year, Philo Farnsworth patented his own electronic television system.

1930
First commercial aired on Charles Jenkins' television program. BBC began its regular TV transmission.

1948
Television hardware became cheaper, enabling one million homes to have one set.

1950-53
FCC approved first two-color television standards.

1956
Introduction of first practical videotape by Ampex and first practical remote control by Robert Adler.

1981
Japanese television company NHK introduced a television system with 1,125 lines of horizontal resolution – the first HD television.

1996
FCC approved modern HDTV standard; one billion television sets in use worldwide.

Adapted from <http://www.television-history.net/television-origin/television-timeline/>. Accessed on March 8, 2019.

3 Decide if the statements are *T* (true) or *F* (false).

a ☐ Electricity made from friction was discovered by count Alessandro Volta.
b ☐ The word "television" was coined when the telephone was invented.
c ☐ The first TV commercial was aired in 1923.
d ☐ Philo Farnsworth introduced the first practical remote control.
e ☐ HD broadcasts were started by a Japanese television company in 1981.

4 Words that are similar in English and in Portuguese are called "cognates". Transcribe the cognates from the text.

_____
_____
_____

5 Match these people and companies to their contribution to the development of television.

a Constantin Perskyi
b Bell Telephone Company
c BBC
d Robert Adler

☐ coined the word "television" during the first International Congress of Electricity in 1900.
☐ introduced the first practical remote control in 1956.
☐ performed the first video image transfer between two cities in 1927.
☐ started its regular TV transmission in 1930.

Post-reading

6 Check the appropriate options.

a The timeline mentions the evolution of television until 1996. What advances have happened since then?
☐ color TV
☐ digital TV
☐ flat-screen TV
☐ HDTV
☐ interactive TV

b In your opinion, what does the future hold for television?
☐ virtual reality TV   ☐ the end of television
☐ holographic TV   ☐ other: _____

7 Do you watch television? If so, how many hours a week?

_____

L2

Toolbox Past simple of regular verbs

1 Read the sentences taken from the timeline in "Explore". Then check the appropriate options.

1775
Count Alessandro Volta **discovered** electricity made from friction.

1981
Japanese television company NHK **introduced** a television system with 1,125 lines of horizontal resolution – the first HD television.

a What function do the highlighted words have in the sentences?
☐ They are nouns.   ☐ They are verbs.

b What do these words have in common?
☐ They end in -ed.   ☐ They have the same meaning.

c Considering that the timeline shows events that happened in a specific period, what is the function of verbs ending in -ed?
☐ To indicate actions in the present.   ☐ To indicate actions in the past.

d Are the examples in the affirmative, negative or interrogative form?
☐ Affirmative form.   ☐ Negative form.   ☐ Interrogative form.

2 Choose the option that describes how the sentences in activity 1 are organized.
a ☐ subject + main verb in the past simple + complement
b ☐ subject + auxiliary verb in the past simple + main verb in the infinitive + complement

3 Read the headline and choose the option that completes each sentence appropriately.

BRUNO MARS 35 things you didn't know about him!

Available at <https://www.uselessdaily.com/news/bruno-mars-35-things-you-didnt-know-about-him-list/#.W3HEppNKhTY>. Accessed on March 11, 2019.

a In the text, the auxiliary verb is _____. The sentence is in the _____.
☐ "did"; affirmative form   ☐ "didn't"; negative form

b It is possible to say that the structure of negative sentences in the past simple is…

☐ subject + auxiliary verb in the past simple ("didn't" or "did not") + complement.

☐ subject + auxiliary verb in the past simple ("didn't" or "did not") + main verb in the infinitive + complement.

4 Read the headline and check the appropriate options.

GOLDEN GLOBES 2018: DID THE RIGHT FILMS WIN?

Available at <http://www.rediff.com/movies/report/golden-globes-2018-did-the-right-films-win-vote/20180108.htm>.
Accessed on March 11, 2019.

a In the text, the auxiliary verb is _____. The sentence is in the _____.

☐ "did"; interrogative form   ☐ "did"; affirmative form

b It is possible to say that the structure of interrogative sentences in the past simple is…

☐ subject + auxiliary verb in the past simple ("did") + main verb in the infinitive + complement.

☐ auxiliary verb in the past simple ("did") + subject + main verb in the infinitive + complement.

5 Complete the sentences using the verbs from the box.

perform (affirmative)   play (affirmative)   play (interrogative)
start (affirmative)   start (negative)   work (affirmative)

a Brazilian actress Alice Braga is famous internationally. She _____ in *I Am Legend* (2007), *Predators* (2010) and *Elysium* (2013).

b Lázaro Ramos _____ his acting career in television. He _____ it in theater.

c American singer Alicia Keys _____ at the Rock in Rio festival, in Rio de Janeiro: in 2013 and in 2017.

d A: _____ Mozart _____ piano when he was a child?

B: Yes, he did. He also _____ many other instruments, including the violin.

6 🎧 12 Listen to the sentences from activity 5 and write each verb in the appropriate column, according to its pronunciation.

-ed pronounced as /d/	-ed pronounced as /t/	-ed pronounced as /ɪd/

L2

Building blocks — Old technology for entertainment

1 Complete these extracts with the name of the devices from the box.

> digital camera   gramophone   MP3 player
> portable cassette player   TV sets   videocassette recorder

a

The first portable _____ that was actually marketed commercially was sold in December 1989 in Japan.

Language clue
1888: eighteen eighty-eight
1989: nineteen eighty-nine
1970s: nineteen-seventies

b

The first working _____ appeared in the 1930s. [...] The first sets could only show black-and-white images.

c

When the _____ (VCR) began to penetrate the mass market in the late 1970s, for the first time consumers were able to store television programming and view it at their convenience.

d

The first generation, playback only, _____ was fragile [...] but in 1979 it had no competition.

e

The first _____ announced was Audio Highway's Listen Up in 1996.

f

On May 16, 1888, [...] Emile Berliner (1851-1929) demonstrated recording and playback on what he called the "_____" at the Franklin Institute in Philadelphia.

Adapted from <https://en.wikipedia.org/wiki/History_of_the_camera>; ***Britannica Student Encyclopedia.*** Edinburgh: Encyclopaedia Britannica, Inc., 2012; <https://www.britannica.com/art/television-in-the-United-States/The-21st-century#ref283658>; BURGESS, Richard James. ***The History of Music Production.*** Oxford: Oxford University Press, 2014. Accessed on March 11, 2019.

2 Based on activity 1, do the following activities.

a Which device(s) did people use to...

I listen to music? _____

II play videos? _____

III take photos? _____

IV watch live programs? _____

b Organize the items depicted in a timeline.

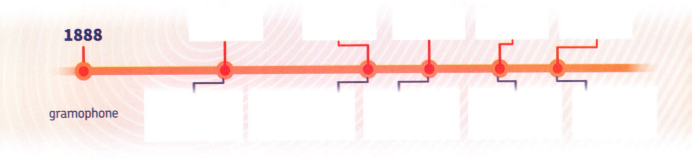

1888 — gramophone

3 Look at the highlighted expressions in activity 1 and read the extract below. Then underline the appropriate prepositions to complete the rules.

"THE WAR OF THE WORLDS" WAS THE 17TH EPISODE OF THE CBS RADIO SERIES *THE MERCURY THEATRE ON THE AIR*, WHICH WAS BROADCAST AT 8 P.M. E.T. ON SUNDAY, OCTOBER 30, 1938.

HOUSEMAN, John. ***Run-Through:* A Memoir**. New York: Simon & Schuster, 1972.

Available at <https://todayinhistory.blog/tag/radio-drama/>. Accessed on March 11, 2019.

a Before months and years, we use **in/on/at**.

b Before dates (month + day; month + day + year), we use **in/on/at**.

c Before time expressions (the 1930s, the late 1970s), we use **in/on/at**.

d Before hours, we use **in/on/at**.

e Before days of the week, we use **in/on/at**.

4 Talk to a partner about your favorite TV program.

a What is your favorite TV show?

b What day is it on?

c What time is it on?

d When did you start watching it?

Listen to: **Entertainment industry**

L3

Sync Listening: Participants' reaction to a game

Pre-listening

1 Look at the pictures and answer the questions.

a What kind of entertainment is represented in the pictures?
_____

b When do you think this kind of entertainment was created?
_____

2 Match the pictures in activity 1 to the type of games they represent.

a ☐ a traditional video game console   c ☐ a computer game
b ☐ a handheld game console   d ☐ a game app

Listening

3 🎧 13 Listen to the first part of an audio with multiple speakers and choose the appropriate options.

a This audio shows _____ a game.
   ☐ the participants' reaction to   ☐ specialists' evaluation about

b The participants are in _____ context.
   ☐ a formal and serious   ☐ an informal and relaxed

c The participants _____ the game.
   ☐ have already played   ☐ have never played

4 🎧14 Listen to part of the audio and underline the appropriate options to complete this extract.

> "In the early 90s, there was a company named **Tiger Electric**/**Lion Electric** that made a bunch of these **handheld**/**PC** games, just like that. And today you are going to experience playing a few of these **new**/**old** popular games."

5 🎧15 Look at the picture and listen to another part of the audio. Which game are the speakers going to play?

A ☐ BASEBALL

B ☐ FOOTBALL

6 🎧16 Listen to the last part of the audio and complete the sentences with the words from the box.

| awful | bad | enjoyable | fun | hard | simple |

Darius: It's actually not as _____ as I thought it would be. I'm actually having a little bit of fun.

Jeannie: Is this _____? I don't... I'm not having fun.

Everhet: It was fun! Actually, it was quite _____! It's a very _____ game, though.

Alix: That was _____. I'm never playing it again.

Reina: You would think that older games and technology would be easier, but... Dang! That was _____.

Post-listening

7 Answer these questions.

a What do you think of this experiment? Was it interesting, funny, curious?

_____

b Would you like to have old kinds of entertainment technologies (portable cassette player, videocassette recorder, old computer)? Why?

_____

L3

Sync Speaking: An interactive presentation about entertainment

Pre-speaking

1 Answer these questions.

a What old entertainment technologies do you know?

_____

b How did you get to know these technologies?

☐ searching on the internet ☐ traveling

☐ talking to my family ☐ watching movies

2 Let's prepare a presentation about an old type of entertainment technology.

a Choose one form of entertainment.

b Research an old technology related to the form of entertainment you have chosen. Discover how and where it was invented, who created it, how it used to work, when it was replaced by another technology or device etc.

c Choose some pictures to illustrate the technology you have chosen. If possible, you can also bring the device itself to enrich your presentation.

d Write a text to help you present the device you have chosen.

e Share your text with a partner and listen to his/her suggestions.

f Revise your text and practice your presentation.

Speaking

3 Present your talk.

a Introduce the device to your classmates and show the pictures you have brought.

b Make some questions about the device to your classmates.

c Talk briefly about the history of the device.

d End your presentation by asking your classmates if they liked the device or not.

Post-speaking

4 Discuss these questions with your classmates.

a Why did you choose to talk about this device?

b How was the research process? What is the most interesting piece of information you found out?

c How was the interaction with your classmates during the presentation?

Studio Timeline

> **What:** a timeline
> **To whom:** students, researchers, people interested in the topic
> **Media:** paper; digital
> **Objective:** show the dates and the order in which significant events related to entertainment happened

1. Search for timelines in English. Take notes of what you find interesting (different layouts, presence of pictures, verb tense used, periods of time mentioned etc.).
2. Choose a topic related to the entertainment world.
3. Research this form of entertainment. Take notes on dates, places, people involved etc. Consult different sources for reliable information.
4. Write a draft of your timeline using the past simple tense.
5. Organize your timeline: highlight the most important events.
6. Share your draft with a partner. Give some suggestions to each other on how to improve your timelines.
7. Revise the text and add some nonverbal elements to your timeline (icons, pictures, drawings etc.).
8. Share your timeline with your classmates.
9. Publish your work on the **Students for PEACE Social Media** <www.studentsforpeace.com.br>, using the tag **timeline** or others chosen by the students.

6 People and their stories

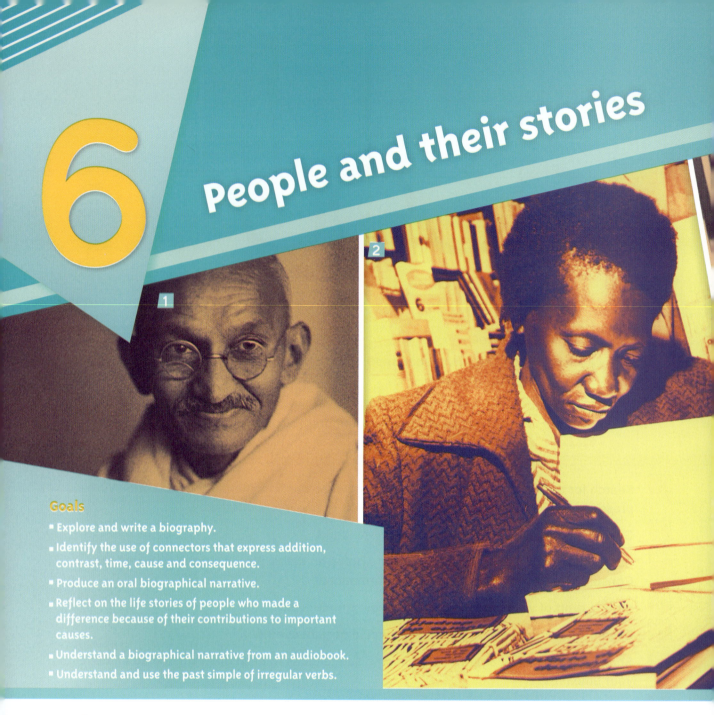

Goals
- Explore and write a biography.
- Identify the use of connectors that express addition, contrast, time, cause and consequence.
- Produce an oral biographical narrative.
- Reflect on the life stories of people who made a difference because of their contributions to important causes.
- Understand a biographical narrative from an audiobook.
- Understand and use the past simple of irregular verbs.

Spark

1 Match these people to the pictures.

a ☐ Albert Einstein   c ☐ Mahatma Gandhi   e ☐ Nelson Mandela
b ☐ Carolina de Jesus d ☐ Marie Curie   f ☐ Rosa Parks

2 How did these people make a difference? Choose the appropriate area(s) from the box.

chemistry   civil rights   law   literature   physics   politics

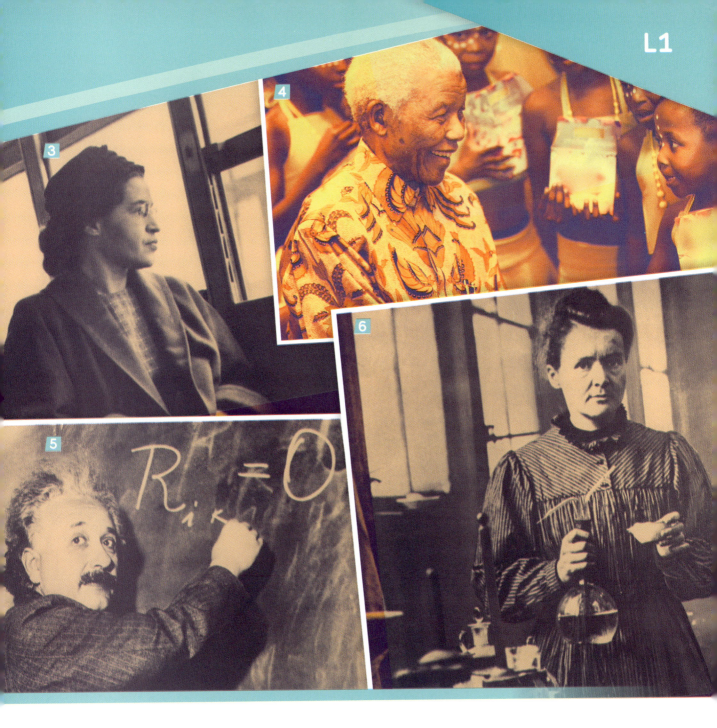

a Albert Einstein: _____

b Carolina de Jesus: _____

c Mahatma Gandhi: _____

d Marie Curie: _____

e Nelson Mandela: _____

f Rosa Parks: _____

3 Do you know other people who have made a difference? Who are/were they?

_____

4 How can you make a difference?

_____

L1

Explore Biography

Pre-reading

1 Look at the pictures and check the appropriate statements.

a ☐ The pictures show book covers about historical figures.

b ☐ The pictures show fiction books.

c ☐ The book covers do not give any suggestion of what these people did.

d ☐ The pictures show covers of biographical books.

e ☐ The books probably tell these people's life stories.

2 What is the difference between a biography and an autobiography? Read the definition and compare it to your answer.

> A narrative that records the actions and recreates the personality of an individual is called a biography (from a Greek term meaning "life-writing"). An individual who writes the story of his or her own life is creating an autobiography, meaning self-biography.

Available at <https://kids.britannica.com/students/article/biography/273218>.
Accessed on March 12, 2019.

3 Take a look at the text in activity 4 and order the topics according to its structure.

a ☐ Fun facts.

b ☐ Introduction to the topic.

c ☐ Title.

d ☐ Professional life and achievements.

e ☐ Personal life.

Reading

4 Read the text and check the only aspect of Einstein's life that is not covered.

Text 1

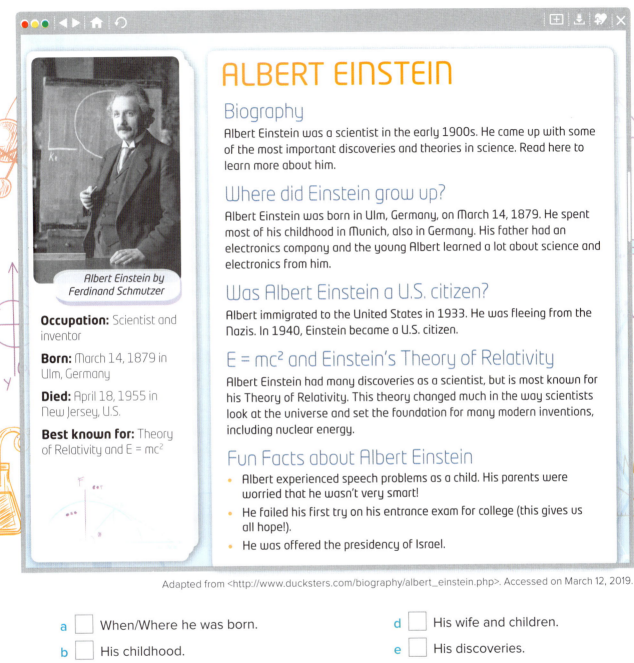

Adapted from <http://www.ducksters.com/biography/albert_einstein.php>. Accessed on March 12, 2019.

a ☐ When/Where he was born.

b ☐ His childhood.

c ☐ The fact that he lived in the United States.

d ☐ His wife and children.

e ☐ His discoveries.

5 Name the section of the text you must read if you want…

a to learn curiosities about Einstein's life: _____

b to read a summary of his biography: _____

c information about Einstein's most important work: _____

d information about his childhood: _____

L1

6 **Answer these questions.**

a What's the title of the text?
_____

b Where was it published?
_____

c What kind of text is this?

☐ an interview   ☐ a biography   ☐ a diary

7 **Read the extract from another biography of Albert Einstein. Then answer the questions.**

Text 2

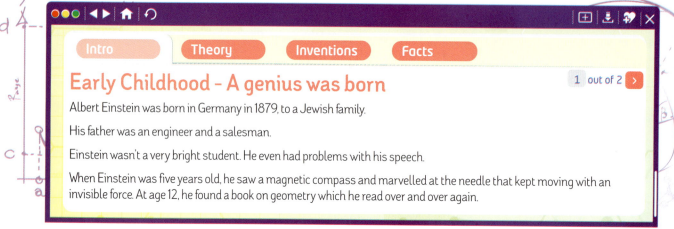

Adapted from <http://mocomi.com/albert-einstein-biography/>. Accessed on March 12, 2019.

a What are the sections of the text?
_____

b How many pages are there in the "Intro" section? _____

8 **Find two differences between texts 1 and 2. Check the appropriate options.**

a ☐ Text 1 is more interactive than text 2.

b ☐ The information mentioned in texts 1 and 2 is totally different.

c ☐ In text 2, the reader can choose what information to read because it is organized into different pages.

d ☐ In text 1, the reader goes from beginning to end in a sequential order.

Post-reading

9 **Discuss the questions with your classmates.**

a Why did the two biographers include similar information in the texts?

b Which biography do you think is more attractive? Why?

Toolbox: Past simple of irregular verbs

1 Read these sentences from the text 1 "Explore" section. Then choose the appropriate options.

"Albert Einstein **was** a scientist in the early 1900s."

"**Was** Albert Einstein a U.S. citizen?"

"His parents **were** worried that he **wasn't** very smart!"

Adapted from <http://www.ducksters.com/biography/albert_einstein.php>. Accessed on March 12, 2019.

a The sentences are in the…

☐ past.   ☐ present.

b The highlighted word in the sentences is the verb…

☐ to be.   ☐ to have.

c To make interrogative and negative sentences with this verb in the past simple, we use…

☐ auxiliary verb in the past simple + main verb in the infinitive + subject (interrogative sentences); subject + verb in the infinitive + "not" (negative sentences).

☐ verb in the past simple + subject (interrogative sentences); subject + verb in the past simple + "not" (negative sentences).

2 Study the sentences in activity 1 and the highlighted excerpts in this text. Then underline the appropriate options.

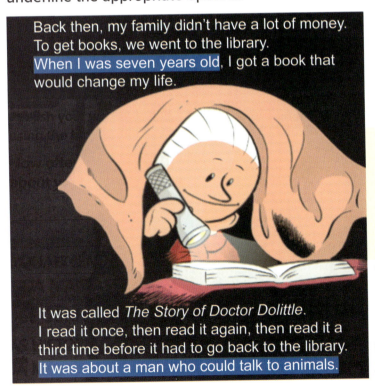

a The verb form "was" is used with "we", "you", "they"/"I", "he", "she", "it".

b The verb form "were" is used with "we", "you", "they"/"I", "he", "she", "it".

MELTZER, Brad; ELIOPOULOS, Christopher. *I Am Jane Goodall.* New York: Dial Books for Young Readers, 2016.

L2

3 Read these extracts focusing on the irregular verbs in the past simple. Then underline the options to make appropriate statements.

> "Where **did** Einstein **grow up**?"

Available at <http://www.ducksters.com/biography/albert_einstein.php>. Accessed on March 12, 2019.

> "[...] My family **didn't have** a lot of money. To get books, we **went** to the library. When I was seven years old, I **got** a book that would change my life. [...] I **read** it once, then **read** it again, then **read** it a third time before it **had** to go back to the library."

MELTZER, Brad; ELIOPOULOS, Christopher. *I Am Jane Goodall.* New York: Dial Books for Young Readers, 2016.

a The past simple of the irregular verbs **is formed/isn't formed** by adding *-ed* to the base form of the verb.

b The auxiliary verb "did" **is/is not** used for both regular and irregular verbs in the negative and interrogative forms.

4 Complete these texts about two notable people with the past simple of the verbs from the box.

a

be (3x)   come   have   see

Caroline Chisolm: a notable Australian woman

One of Australia's most notable women _____ Caroline Chisholm. She was born in England in 1808 and _____ to Australia in 1838. She _____ that many immigrants _____ poor and _____ no place to live, so she helped them get jobs and homes. Her portrait _____ on the Australian five-dollar bill for many years.

Adapted from <http://www.kidcyber.com.au/caroline-chisolm/>. Accessed on March 12, 2019.

b

be (2x)   become   have   read   speak

Machado de Assis: a 19th century Brazilian writer ahead of his time

Machado de Assis _____ a Brazilian novelist, poet, playwright and short story writer. He _____ French, English, German and Greek. His work didn't gain popularity abroad during his lifetime, but he eventually _____ known outside Brazil. Many famous writers have honored Machado de Assis by including him among the greatest 100 geniuses of literature. I _____ a wonderful Portuguese teacher. He introduced me to Machado de Assis. The first three books I _____ _____ *Dom Casmurro* (*Sir Dour*), *Memórias póstumas de Brás Cubas* (*Epitaph for a Small Winner*) and *O alienista* (*The Alienist* or *The Psychiatrist*).

Adapted from <https://streetsmartbrazil.com/machado-de-assis-19th-century-brazilian-writer-ahead-his-time/>. Accessed on March 12, 2019.

Building blocks Connectors (linking words)

1 Read this biography and guess who it is about.

He enjoyed Math **and** Science at school, where he earned the nickname "Einstein". He wanted to study Math at university **but** Oxford didn't have a Math degree at the time, **so** he chose Physics and Chemistry.

After graduation, he went to Cambridge to study for his PhD. He began to have health issues. Doctors discovered that he had a progressive neurodegenerative disease called ALS. They said he only had a few years to live. He wanted to earn his PhD **before** he died. Despite the initial diagnosis, he lived a full and productive life with the help of science and modern medicine.

Perhaps his most famous discovery was when he demonstrated that black holes emit some radiation. Prior to this, it was thought that black holes could not get smaller **because** nothing could escape their enormous gravity.

2 Complete the definitions with the highlighted connectors from activity 1.

a _____: used to mention something that occurred at an earlier time.

b _____: used to express contrast.

c _____: used to mention something that occurred at a later time.

d _____: used to add ideas.

e _____: used to explain the cause of something.

f _____: used to express that something occurred as a result of something else.

3 Read this extract from a biography of Rosa Parks and complete the gaps with the appropriate connectors.

Biography
Rosa Parks

Rosa Parks is famous for her refusal, on December 1, 1955, to obey bus driver James Blake's demand that she relinquish her seat to a white man. Her subsequent arrest _____ trial for this act of civil disobedience triggered the Montgomery Bus Boycott, one of the largest and most successful mass movements against racial segregation in history.

"People always say that I didn't give up my seat _____ I was tired, _____ that isn't true. I was not tired physically. No, the only tired I was, was tired of giving in."

Adapted from <https://www.biographyonline.net/humanitarian/rosa-parks.html>. Accessed on March 12, 2019.

L3

Sync Listening: **An audiobook extract**

Pre-listening

1 Answer these questions.

a What is an audiobook?

_____

b Who is the intended audience for an audiobook?

_____

_____

2 Look at the pictures and read the texts.

By: Ann Abramson

Narrated by: Kevin Pariseau

Length: 44 min.

Unabridged audiobook

Release date: 03-25-09

Language: English

★★★★½ 4.6 (90 ratings)

Adapted from <https://www.audible.com.au/pd/Children/Who-Was-Anne-Frank-Audiobook/B00FNZ638A>. Accessed on March 12, 2019.

Who Was Anne Frank?

☐ A high-spirited child always playing pranks

☐ A young Jewish girl forced into hiding for two years

☐ The author of one of the best-loved books in the world

☑ All of the above!

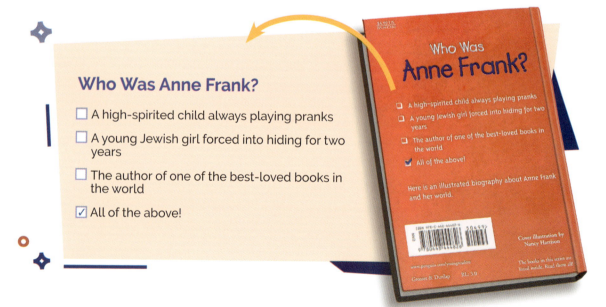

3 Now answer the questions about *Who Was Anne Frank?* audiobook.

a What's the title?

b Who wrote it?

c Who narrates the story?

d How long is the story?

e When was it published?

f Did listeners consider it a good audiobook?

Listening

4 🎧 17 Listen to an extract of *Who Was Anne Frank?*. What subjects about Anne does it cover?

- a ☐ her date of birth
- b ☐ her place of birth
- c ☐ her brother's name
- d ☐ her parents' names
- e ☐ her personality traits
- f ☐ her pets' names
- g ☐ her physical appearance
- h ☐ her favorite sport

5 🎧 18 Listen to the first part of the narrative again. Then circle the appropriate options.

a Anne was born on June 12, **1929/1939**.

b She was from **Britain/Germany**.

c Her father's name was **Walter/Otto** and her mother's name was **Edith/Margot**.

d Anne **had/didn't have** a sister.

e They lived in **Frankfurt/London**.

f Their apartment **wasn't/was** full of books.

Post-listening

6 Discuss these questions with your classmates.

a If you had to live hiding from someone, like Anne did, do you think you would start writing a diary? Why?

b In your opinion, why is Anne's diary considered an important document for history?

L3

Sync Speaking: A biographical narrative

Pre-speaking

1 Write a short biography of an inspirational person you know. Follow the instructions.

a In groups, choose someone that you all consider inspiring for some reason.

b Make a list of things you would like to know about him/her.

c Search for information about him/her.

d Write the biography, including the title and the authors. Use a dictionary if necessary.

e Share your draft with another group.

f Revise your text.

g Add some pictures to your text.

h Rehearse narrating the biography.

Speaking

2 You are going to record the biography you wrote and present it to the whole class.

a Start your recording saying the title of the biography and its authors.

b Narrate the biography.

c In the classroom, make a circle with all groups together and play the recordings.

d Discuss with the class the biographies you listened.

Post-speaking

3 Answer these questions.

a How was the research process? What sources were consulted?

b How did you feel narrating the biography?

 Studio Biography

What: a short biography
To whom: other students; the school community
Media: paper; digital
Objective: inform readers about the life story of an important person

1. In groups, choose a relevant historical figure (in science, politics, human rights, medicine, arts etc.).
2. Search for pieces of information about this person.
3. Write the biography. Organize it into topics or sections.
4. Share your draft with other groups.
5. Revise your text.
6. Choose a picture of the person you are writing about. Add a caption to it.
7. Share the biography with your classmates.
8. Gather all the biographies and create a biography book.
9. Publish your work on the **Students for PEACE Social Media** <www.studentsforpeace.com.br>, using the tag **biography** or others chosen by the students.

Peace talk

Chapters 5 and 6
Once upon a real time...

1 Answer the questions and discuss them with your classmates.

a Você conhece alguém ou se lembra de algum acontecimento cuja relevância justificaria sua representação cinematográfica? Se sim, por quê?

_____

b O que faz uma história real merecer ser transformada em um filme que, depois de pronto, possa servir de inspiração para muitas pessoas?

_____

c Você já assistiu a algum filme baseado em fatos reais? Na sua opinião, nesse/s filme/s, o que era real e o que foi adicionado por iniciativa dos/as produtores/produtoras? Por que isso teria acontecido?

_____

2 Read the synopses of three movies that were inspired by real events. Then complete the sentences with the title of these movies.

1

A five-year-old Indian boy gets lost on the streets of Kolkata, thousands of kilometers from home. He survives many challenges before being adopted by a couple in Australia. Twenty-five years later, he sets out to find his lost family.

Adapted from <https://www.imdb.com/title/tt3741834/>. Accessed on May 31, 2019.

2

Young Bruno lives a wealthy lifestyle in pre-war Germany along with his mother, elder sister and SS Commandant father. The family relocates to the countryside, where his father is assigned to take command of a prison camp. A few days later, Bruno befriends another youth, strangely dressed in striped pajamas, named Shmuel, who lives behind an electrified fence. Bruno will soon find out that he is not permitted to befriend his new friend as he is a Jew, and that the neighboring yard is actually a prison camp for Jews awaiting extermination.

Based on <https://www.imdb.com/title/tt0914798/>. Accessed on May 31, 2019.

As the United States raced against Russia to put a man in space, NASA found untapped talent in a group of African-American female mathematicians that served as the brains behind one of the greatest operations in the U.S. history. Based on the unbelievably true life stories of three of these women, known as "human computers".

Adapted from <https://www.imdb.com/title/tt4846340/>. Accessed on May 31, 2019.

a O filme que conta a história de um grupo de mulheres negras à frente de seu tempo no campo científico nos Estados Unidos da década de 1960, durante a Guerra Fria, é _____.

b O filme que conta a história de uma pessoa que tenta reencontrar sua família após mais de duas décadas é _____.

c O filme que conta uma história fictícia sobre a amizade entre duas crianças durante um acontecimento histórico real da humanidade, marcado pela intolerância extrema (os campos de concentração na Alemanha nazista, durante a Segunda Guerra Mundial), é _____.

3 **Refer to the movies in activity 2 and discuss these questions with your classmates.**

a Você já assistiu a algum desses filmes? Em caso afirmativo, qual deles? Qual foi sua opinião? Em caso negativo, ficou interessado/a em assistir a algum?

b Pensando no conceito de Cultura de Paz, qual/quais desses filmes, na sua opinião, poderia/m ser tomado/s como representativo/s dos seguintes pilares dessa cultura?

I Igualdade
II Solidariedade
III Direitos Humanos
IV Participação democrática

4 **Plan an occasion to hear real stories in the classroom. Follow the instructions.**

a Façam um levantamento sobre pessoas mais velhas que tenham boas histórias verdadeiras para contar. Pensem em seus pais, avós, outros/as parentes, vizinhos/as etc.

b Calculem o tempo de uma aula e verifiquem quantas pessoas poderiam participar de uma roda de conversa para contar suas histórias considerando, por exemplo, que cada história poderia ser contada num tempo médio de dez minutos. Considerem também um tempo para perguntas.

c Se sua turma se organizar em grupos, cada grupo pode trazer um/a convidado/a.

d Verifiquem se as pessoas escolhidas para contar as histórias poderiam comparecer à escola. É possível também fazer o registro das histórias em vídeo.

e Façam o convite aos/às participantes e preparem a recepção de cada um/a deles/delas.

f Aproveitem para conhecer a história de vida dessas pessoas. Divirtam-se e emocionem-se!

g Enquanto ouvem as histórias, anotem os fatos que acharem mais interessantes ou emocionantes. Ao final, compartilhem suas impressões sobre as histórias.

7 History is all around us

1. Monumento Nacional ao Imigrante (Caxias do Sul, RS)
2. Museu de Arte Contemporânea (Niterói, RJ)

Goals
- Explore encyclopedia entries.
- Recognize different kinds of landmarks.
- Think about the importance of history.
- Understand and create an oral narrative.
- Understand and use the past continuous to describe events that were in progress at a certain time in the past.
- Write an encyclopedia entry.

Spark

1 Take a look at the pictures and match the landmarks to their purposes.

a ☐ To honor a group of people.
b ☐ To connect two parts of the city.
c ☐ To honor a notable person.
d ☐ To preserve history and culture.

> **Language clue**
> **Landmark** is a construction or monument of historical importance.

Zumbi dos Palmares (Brasília, DF)

Viaduto do Chá (São Paulo, SP)

2 Read the statements and write *T* (true) or *F* (false).

a ☐ The monument in picture 1 honors the Brazilian people.
b ☐ The museum in picture 2 presents works of art from the Brazilian culture.
c ☐ The sculpture presented in picture 3 mentions detailed information about Zumbi's life.
d ☐ In picture 4, the viaduct's name is a tribute to the history of the place, where there used to be a tea plantation.

3 Are there any landmarks in your city? Write their names and describe them.

_____
_____

L1

Explore Encyclopedia entry

Pre-reading

1 Discuss the questions with your classmates.

a Have you ever been to a library? What did you research? What kind of books did you consult?

b Have you ever used the internet to do some research? What kind of websites did you consult?

2 What are the differences between using a book and the internet to research? Check the appropriate options.

a ☐ There is not reliable information on the internet.

b ☐ When using the internet, we can find the information we want by typing a keyword related to the topic of the research.

c ☐ In a book, we have to use the contents or the index to find the topic we are looking for.

d ☐ Books can be updated as fast as websites.

Reading

3 Look at the text. What kind of text is it?

_____

Text 1

A
B

192
Belau >> Belgrade

Belau See PALAU

Belém \be-'lem\ City (pop., 2000 prelim.: metro. area, 1,271,615), northern Brazil. The capital of Pará state, the port of Belém lies on the Pará River in the vast AMAZON RIVER delta 90 mi (145 km) from the Atlantic Ocean. It began in 1616 as a fortified settlement; as it gradually became established, it helped consolidate Portuguese supremacy in northern Brazil. It was made the state capital in 1772. It enjoyed prosperity in the late 19th century as the main exporting centre of the Amazon rubber industry. After the rubber era ended in 1912, it continued to be northern Brazil's commercial centre and a main port for Amazon River craft.

belemnoid \'bel-əm-,nòid\ or **belemnite** Member of an extinct group of CEPHALOPODS, possessing a large internal shell, that first appeared c. 345 million years ago, in the Early CARBONIFEROUS PERIOD, and became extinct during the EOCENE EPOCH, which ended c. 36.6 million years ago. The internal shell of most species is straight, but that of some species is loosely coiled. The shell served for support and muscle attachment and enabled the animal to compensate for depth and its own body weight. See also AMMONOID.

Reconstruction of squidlike belemnoid cephalopods from the Cretaceous System, southern Tennessee
COURTESY OF THE AMERICAN MUSEUM OF NATURAL HISTORY, NEW YORK

Britannica Concise Encyclopedia. Encyclopaedia Britannica Inc., 2008. p. 192.

4 Read the text and check the appropriate options.

a The entries (terms defined on the page) are organized…

☐ in alphabetical order.
☐ in topics.

b The entries _____ about one specific school subject (e.g., Biology, History, Geography).

☐ are
☐ are not

c The visual elements are used to…

☐ complement some of the entries.
☐ anticipate the entries that will appear on the following page.

d The words that appear in the header of the page ("Belau >> Belgrade") indicate that the entries on the page are _____ these two words in alphabetical order.

☐ between
☐ before and after

e To read about Belau, we have to look for the word _____ in the encyclopedia.

☐ see
☐ Palau

5 Find the abbreviations for these words in the entry "Belém".

a population: _____
b preliminary: _____
c metropolitan: _____
d miles: _____
e kilometers: _____

6 Complete the chart about Belém with information from the text.

Items	Notes
How to pronounce "Belém"	
Geographical position	
State that the city of Belém belongs to	
The date it was founded	

> **Going further**
> Belém was founded in the province of Grão-Pará.
> The word "Pará" means "big river" in Tupi-Guarani.

L1

7 Read this entry about the city of Recife and write *T* (true) or *F* (false).

Text 2

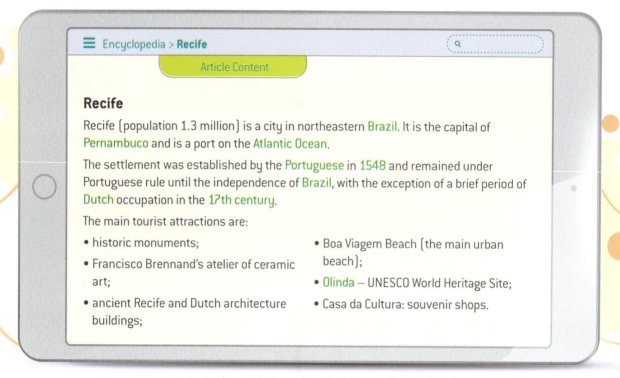

Adapted from <http://encyclopedia.kids.net.au/page/re/Recife>. Accessed on March 18, 2019.

a ☐ The page presents only one entry.
b ☐ There is no information about the history of the city and its location.
c ☐ The information presented may be relevant for tourists.
d ☐ From this entry, it is possible to look for information about Brazil, the Atlantic Ocean and the city of Olinda.

8 Compare the entries for the two cities and write *T1* for text 1 and *T2* for text 2.

a ☐ Which entry(ies) may be more helpful for someone who wants to visit the city?
b ☐ Which entry(ies) may be more helpful for someone who wants to write a History paper about the city?
c ☐ Which entry(ies) present(s) information and narrate(s) facts?

Post-reading

9 Discuss the questions with a partner.

a If you had to rewrite these encyclopedia entries, what other pieces of information would you add? Would you delete anything?
b Is there any place you would like to know more about? Would you use an encyclopedia or a website to research about it? Why?

Building blocks — Landmarks

1 Read this extract from an encyclopedia entry. Then name two examples of famous landmarks.

> **Landmarks** are permanent structures such as trees, bridges, buildings and statues that contribute to the historic, cultural or architectural heritage of a city.

MISIROGLU, Gina. *The Handy Answer Book for Kids (and Parents).* Canton: Visible Ink Press, 2009. p. 112.

2 Match these words to the pictures.

a church   b monument   c palace   d park   e port   f square

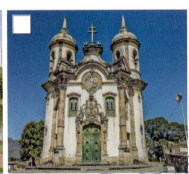

3 Can the pictures in activity 2 be considered landmarks? Why?

4 Think about your city and choose one of its landmarks to describe to a partner.

> **Useful language**
> There's a/an…
> It's called…
> It celebrates/represents/honors…
> I like/don't like it because…

L2

Toolbox Past continuous

1 Look at the picture of an American Civil War landmark. Then read the excerpts and write *T* (true) or *F* (false).

Going further

The **American Civil War** (1861-1865) was the war between the North and the South of the United States. The southern states, known as the Confederates, tried to separate from the rest of the country because they did not want to give up the slave labor in their fields.

Text 1

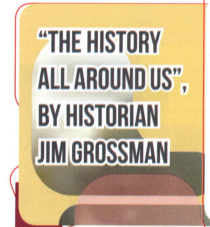

"THE HISTORY ALL AROUND US", BY HISTORIAN JIM GROSSMAN

There are many ways in which people encounter history in public places. Every southern county seat has a monument of a Confederate soldier. Why are they there? What was the meaning of that monument when it was built? How did that meaning change over the time? Was that Confederate soldier defending the honor, the tradition or the ownership of one human being by another? These are interesting questions. They are ethical questions, they are political questions. And any historian can open a conversation about this in their community.

Adapted from <https://www.youtube.com/watch?v=NgAER9GS3OQ>. Accessed on March 19, 2019.

Text 2

About the Civil War, by Alfred Hornung

In their obstinate insistence to preserve what should not be preserved, Confederate soldiers were not fighting in the name of humanistic values.

HORNUNG, Alfred. ***Intercultural America.*** Heidelberg: Winter, 2007. p. 182.

a ☐ Both excerpts are related to the American Civil War.
b ☐ According to text 1, people should ask some questions when visiting a historic landmark.
c ☐ Jim Grossman answers the questions he makes.
d ☐ Text 2 presents different perspectives of the American Civil War.
e ☐ According to Alfred Hornung, the Confederate soldiers' fight was not right or fair.

2. Analyze these sentences from the texts. Then check the appropriate options.

> "**Was** that Confederate soldier **defending** the honor, the tradition or the ownership of one human being by another?"

> "[...] Confederate soldiers **were not fighting** in the name of humanistic values."

a. The excerpts refer to the...
- [ ] past.
- [ ] present.

b. The actions...
- [ ] were in progress for a certain time.
- [ ] happened (or didn't happen) at once.

c. The auxiliary verb used is _____ and the ending of the main verb is _____.
- [ ] "did"; -ed.
- [ ] "was"/"were"; -ing.

d. In the negative form, "not" is used...
- [ ] before the auxiliary verb.
- [ ] after the auxiliary verb.

e. In the interrogative form, "was"/"were" is used...
- [ ] before the subject.
- [ ] after the subject.

f. Based on the rules, the structure of affirmative sentences in the past continuous is...
- [ ] subject + auxiliary verb in the past simple ("was"/"were") + complement.
- [ ] subject + auxiliary verb in the past simple ("was"/"were") + main verb with -ing + complement.

3. Read these sentences and check the appropriate timelines according to them.

a. Dom Pedro II was ruling **when** Deodoro da Fonseca, Marshal of the army, established a federal republic in 1889.

Adapted from <http://encyclopedia.kids.net.au/page/hi/History_of_Brazil?title=Dom_Joao_VI>. Accessed on March 19, 2019.

b. Regent Princess Isabel abolished slavery in 1888 **while** Dom Pedro II was traveling.

Adapted from <http://encyclopedia.kids.net.au/page/hi/History_of_Brazil?title=Dom_Joao_VI>. Accessed on March 19, 2019.

4. According to your answers in activity 3, match the words to their meanings.

a. while
b. when

- [ ] at a certain moment
- [ ] during the time that; at the same time as

L3

Sync Listening: Immigration

Pre-listening

1 Match the pictures to the captions.

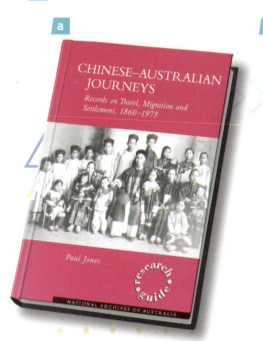

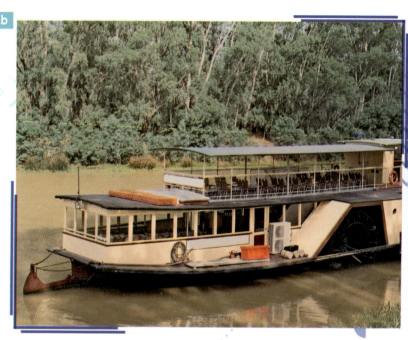

☐ A book about the Chinese migration to Australia.

☐ A map of Australia.

☐ A paddle steamer on the Murray River, Australia.

2 Based on the pictures in activity 1, check the options you think the audio is going to talk about.

a ☐ Chinese immigration.
b ☐ Australia and its native people.
c ☐ Australian cities.
d ☐ The Chinese community in Australia.

Listening

3 🎧19 Listen to this narrative and check the appropriate options.

a ☐ The girl's name is Mary.
b ☐ She is talking about her grandfather.
c ☐ She tells the story of John Egge.
d ☐ She talks about Chinese immigration.

4 🎧19 Listen to the narrative again. Then number the topics according to the order in which they are mentioned.

a ☐ Summary of the life of the person she is talking about.
b ☐ Name and origin of the person she is talking about.
c ☐ Name of the person who is telling the story.
d ☐ Contributions of immigrants to her country's culture.
e ☐ Facts about the history of immigration in her country.

5 🎧19 Listen to the audio and underline the appropriate options to complete the sentences.

a John Egge came to Australia from China in **1851/1852**.
b **Many/A few** Chinese people immigrated to Australia in the 19th century.
c Chinese immigrants worked in **Victoria's/Melbourne's** goldfields, so they could make money to send back to their families.
d Chinese traditions **are/are not** still alive in Australia.

Post-listening

6 Discuss these questions with your classmates.

a Take a look at the previous activities. Which pieces of information about Australia are new to you?
b Is it important that people know about their origins? How can they find this kind of information?

L3

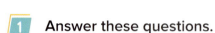 **Speaking: A narrative about people and their history**

Pre-speaking

1 Answer these questions.

a Where are you from? Where is your family from?

b Which groups had an important role in the history of your city/state? What do you know about these groups of people?

2 Let's prepare a presentation about a relative or a historic figure from your city/state.

a Choose someone who belongs to one of the groups you've mentioned in activity 1.

b Research and take notes. Then write a text presenting this person and his/her story.

c Gather the classmates who are writing about people from the same group. Share your text with them. Exchange suggestions about each other's work.

d Revise your text.

e Research with your group: what is the story of this people's group in your city/state?

f Organize your presentation into topics: write an introduction, collect the texts and add some information about the group of people chosen and its contributions.

g Add some visual elements to your presentation if possible (objects, clothing, traditional food and/or pictures).

h Decide who is going to be responsible for each part of the presentation and practice it.

Speaking

3 Present your talk. Then check if your classmates have questions about it.

Post-speaking

4 Answer these questions.

a Why did you choose to talk about this particular person and this group?

b How did you feel when talking to your classmates? Use the words from the box.

> anxious   calm   confident   nervous

96

Studio | Encyclopedia entry

> **What:** an encyclopedia entry
> **To whom:** other students; the school community
> **Media:** paper; digital
> **Objective:** inform readers about the history of landmarks

1. List the characteristics of an encyclopedia entry.
2. Work in groups. Choose one historic landmark in your city/state. Which pieces of information would be interesting to know about this landmark?
3. Research and take notes.
4. Choose some topics and subtopics for your encyclopedia entry. Then write your text.
5. Add some pictures that can give some visual support to your entry. Then organize the layout.
6. Share your entry with other groups and ask for their feedback. Give them some suggestions as well.
7. Revise your text.
8. Share your work with your classmates and teacher.
9. Gather all the entries and organize them to create an encyclopedia. Share it in your school library.
10. Publish your work on the **Students for PEACE Social Media** <www.studentsforpeace.com.br>, using the tag **encyclopediaentry** or others chosen by the students.

8 When I was a kid

Goals
- Explore and write a blog post.
- Review and contrast the use of the past simple and the past continuous.
- Review some connectors.
- Talk about different kinds of games.
- Understand and share childhood memories.
- Understand and use the modal verb "could" to describe abilities in the past.
- Understand and use "used to" to talk about habits in the past.

Spark

 Take a look at the pictures. What are these kids doing? Match the pictures to the descriptions.

a ☐ They are studying at school.
b ☐ She is relaxing and having fun with her family.
c ☐ They are playing hide-and-seek.
d ☐ She is playing and using her imagination.
e ☐ They are having lunch with their family.

L1

2 Which do you prefer: indoor or outdoor activities? Why?

_____

3 According to the pictures, it is possible to say that...
   a ☐ kids should have a healthy and balanced diet.
   b ☐ children need to have a lot of toys to be happy.
   c ☐ kids need to study in order to have a healthy childhood.
   d ☐ children should always have an activity to be done: they shouldn't rest and relax.

L1

Explore Blog post

Pre-reading

1 Do the following activities.

a Have you ever followed a blog? If so, what was it about? Check the theme/s.
- [ ] books
- [ ] games
- [ ] movies and television
- [ ] music
- [ ] science and curiosities
- [ ] others: _____

b In your opinion, why do people decide to create a blog? Check the answers.
- [ ] To express themselves.
- [ ] To make people laugh.
- [ ] To support an important cause.
- [ ] To make new friends.
- [ ] To study more and learn new things.
- [ ] Others: _____

2 What do you know about blogs? Write *T* (true) or *F* (false).

a ☐ You can edit the blog posts after posting them.
b ☐ You can't choose the posts you want to read in a blog.
c ☐ Posts usually have the date and time of publication and are displayed from the most recent to the oldest.
d ☐ Readers can never comment on posts.
e ☐ Blog layouts can be personalized.

3 What do you know about Malala Yousafzai? Skim the text in activity 4 and check the words you think will appear in it.

a ☐ death
b ☐ firing
c ☐ future
d ☐ games
e ☐ homework
f ☐ liberty
g ☐ movies
h ☐ peace
i ☐ playground
j ☐ shopping mall

Going further

Malala Yousafzai was born in Pakistan in 1997. She started writing a blog for BBC in which she described her life under the Taliban rule. She won the Nobel Peace Prize when she was only 17.

Reading

4 Read the text. Then check your answers to activity 3.

Malala's diary

Wednesday 18 February
I went to the market today. It was crowded. People are happy about the deal. I saw a traffic jam after a long time. In the evening my father broke the news of the death of a Swat journalist (Musa Khankhel). Our hopes of peace have been smashed.

Sunday 15 February
My father told me that he read in the newspaper that the government and the militants are to sign a peace deal tomorrow and the firing is in jubilation.

Thursday 12 February
There was heavy shelling last night. Both my brothers were sleeping, but I could not. I went to lie down with my father, but then I went to my mother, but could not sleep. That was why I also woke up late in the morning. In the afternoon I had tuition. In the evening I continued playing with my brothers. Also played games on the computer for a while.

Wednesday 14 January
I was in a bad mood while going to school because winter vacations are starting from tomorrow. The principal announced the vacations but did not mention the date the school was to reopen. Since today was the last day of our school, we decided to play in the playground a bit longer.

Monday 5 January
I was getting ready for school and about to wear my uniform when I remembered that our principal had told us not to wear uniforms – and come to school wearing normal clothes instead. So I decided to wear my favourite pink dress. Other girls in school were also wearing colourful dresses.

Sunday 4 January
Today is a holiday and I woke up late, around 10 a.m. Before the launch of the military operation, we all used to go to Marghazar, Fiza Ghat and Kanju for picnics on Sundays. But now the situation is such that we have not been out on a picnic for over a year and a half. We also used to go for a walk after dinner, but now we are back home before sunset. Today I did some household chores, my homework and played with my brother. But my heart was beating fast – as I have to go to school tomorrow.

Saturday 3 January
I had a terrible dream yesterday with military helicopters and the Taliban. My mother made me breakfast and I went off to school. I was afraid of going to school because the Taliban had issued an edict banning all girls from attending schools.

Adapted from <http://www.bbc.com/news/world-asia-29565738>. Accessed on March 26, 2019.

5 Read the questions and check the appropriate options.

a Who wrote the text?

☐ Malala's father.   ☐ Malala.

b Why did Malala describe going to the market?

☐ Because it was her favorite place to go during the war.
☐ Because she wanted to show that life was getting back to normal.

c Why was Malala afraid of going to school?

☐ Because girls were prohibited from attending school.
☐ Because she didn't like school.

L1

6 Read the text again and match each picture to a date, according to the blog posts.

a
b
c
d
e
f

☐ 3 January ☐ 12 February ☐ 5 January
☐ 4 January ☐ 14 January ☐ 18 February

Post-reading

7 If you decided to write about a problem related to kids, what issue would it be about? Check the possible options.

☐ Bullying at school.
☐ Violence against children.
☐ Kids around the world who are hungry.
☐ Forced child labor.
☐ Kids who are out of school.
☐ Other: _____

8 Malala mentions some activities she used to do for fun. Are they similar to what you like doing in your free time? Explain your answer.

Toolbox: Past simple, past continuous and "could"

1 Read the sentences from Malala's blog and complete the statements.

a "My mother **made** me breakfast and I **went** off to school."
b "Other girls in school **were** also **wearing** colourful dresses."
c "Both my brothers **were sleeping**, but I could not."
d "Today I **did** some household chores, my homework and **played** with my brother."

I Sentences _____ describe events that happened at a specific moment in the past.

II Sentences _____ describe events that were in progress during a certain time in the past.

2 Answer these questions with information about yourself.

a What were you doing at 5:30 a.m. today?

b What were you doing at 7 p.m. yesterday?

c What were you doing last Sunday morning?

d What did you do last Saturday?

e What did you do today before you came to school?

f What did you learn last year about technology?

3 Read the excerpt from the text and check the appropriate options.

> "There was heavy shelling last night. Both my brothers were sleeping, but I **could not**. I went to lie down with my father, but then I went to my mother, but **could not** sleep."

a In the excerpt, "could not" means...
- [ ] Malala shouldn't sleep because she had to protect her brothers.
- [ ] Malala didn't want to sleep because she wasn't sleepy.
- [ ] Malala tried to sleep, but she wasn't able to.

b Why couldn't she sleep?
- [ ] Because she wasn't sleepy.
- [ ] Because of the bombs.
- [ ] Because nobody was sleeping.

L2

4 Make questions about your classmates' abilities in the past. Find someone who could do these things. Follow the examples.

> COULD YOU SWIM WHEN YOU WERE A SMALL KID?
>
> YES, I COULD.

> COULD YOU RIDE A BIKE WHEN YOU WERE A SMALL CHILD?
>
> NO, I COULDN'T.

Find someone who could...

a play an instrument: _____

b swim: _____

c sing: _____

d read: _____

e ride a bike: _____

f jump rope: _____

> **Going further**
>
> We use "can" to talk about an ability someone has in the present. "Could" is used to talk about abilities in the past: "Mozart **could** play the piano very well".

5 Read these excerpts from Malala's blog. Then match them to the following statements about the words in bold.

a "[...] I remembered that our principal had told us not to wear uniforms – and come to school wearing normal clothes instead. **So** I decided to wear my favourite pink dress."

b "My mother made me breakfast **and** I went off to school."

c "Before the launch of the military operation, we all used to go to Marghazar, Fiza Ghat and Kanju for picnics on Sundays. **But** now the situation is such that we have not been out on a picnic for over a year and a half."

d "I went to lie down with my father, but **then** I went to my mother, but could not sleep."

☐ This word expresses addition. It is used to connect two events.

☐ This word expresses contrast: something was expected, but the opposite happened.

☐ This word expresses a result: something happened and caused an impact on a following event.

☐ This word is used to talk about an action that happened in a sequence of another one. One of its synonyms is "next".

Building blocks Games

1 Look at the pictures and check the games you used to play when you were a child.

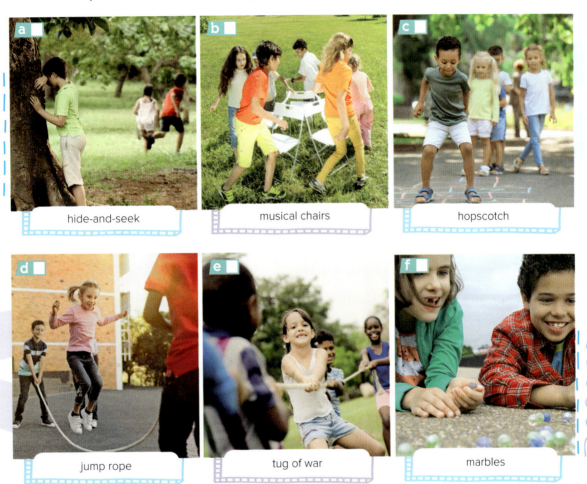

a. hide-and-seek
b. musical chairs
c. hopscotch
d. jump rope
e. tug of war
f. marbles

2 Match the games from activity 1 to their descriptions.

☐ It is a game played with small glass balls. Kids usually collect them and there are many ways to play it. One of them is trying to hit the opponent's balls out of a circle on the ground.

☐ In order to play this game, you have to set up chairs in a circle (one less than the amount of people playing the game). When the music starts, the players start walking around the chairs. When the music stops, the person who did not find a seat is out of the game.

☐ This game needs two teams playing against each other, pulling at opposite ends of a rope. The objective is to pull the rope over a mark on the ground.

☐ The players have to jump over a rope swung under their feet and over their heads.

☐ The players make a grid on the floor using some chalk. They number the squares from one to nine and find a small rock. Then they toss the rock onto the squares and jump in order to take the same rock.

☐ One player is called "IT" (the seeker), who has to count to 10, while the other players hide; at the end of the count, he/she tries to find all the others. The last player to be found becomes "IT" for the next round.

3 Read these excerpts from Malala's blog. Then underline the appropriate options.

> "[...] we [...] used to go to Marghazar, Fiza Ghat and Kanju for picnics on Sundays. But now the situation is such that we have not been out on a picnic for over a year and a half."
>
> "We [...] used to go for a walk after dinner, but now we are back home before sunset."

a "Used to" refers to habits in the **present/past** that don't happen anymore.

b In the negative form, we use **"don't use to"/"didn't use to"**.

c To ask questions, we use **"did" + subject + "use to" + verb/"do" + subject + "use to" + verb**.

4 Look at the pictures and answer the questions with information about yourself. Then ask the same questions to a partner.

a seesaw
b jungle gym
c monkey bars
d slide
e swings
f roundabout

a Did you use to go on the seesaw when you were a small kid?
_____

b Did you use to climb the jungle gym when you were a small child?
_____

c Did you use to play on the monkey bars when you were younger?
_____

d Did you use to go down the slide when you were little?
_____

e Did you use to play on the swings when you were a baby?
_____

f Did you use to go on the roundabout when you were younger?
_____

Sync Listening: What's your favorite childhood memory?

Pre-listening

1 Check the possible options. Then share your answers with your classmates.

a Do you have good childhood memories? Who was with you in these memories?

- [ ] my family
- [ ] my friends
- [ ] my pets
- [ ] others: _____

b Why do you think they have become special memories?

- [ ] Because of the place I was at.
- [ ] Because of the people who were with me.
- [ ] Because of the lessons I learned.
- [ ] Because of the things I did.

Listening

2 🎧 Listen to four people talking about their favorite childhood memories. Then order the memories from 1 to 4.

a [ ] Moments with her grandmother.
b [ ] Being at the hospital with other kids.
c [ ] Making friends at school.
d [ ] The first magic trick for the family and friends.

3 🎧 Listen to the audio again. Then check the reasons why the people chose these memories.

a In audio 1, the person talks about learning to do magic tricks because...
- [ ] he wanted to be a famous magician.
- [ ] he made his family and friends laugh.

b In audio 2, the person talks about spending time with her grandmother because...
- [ ] she used to tell stories about her childhood and about her parents.
- [ ] she used to take her to nice places.

c Why did the person in audio 3 make so many friends at school?
- [ ] Because he was an extrovert and had a lot of fun with his classmates.
- [ ] Because the kids at school wanted to sign the plaster cast on his arms.

d The person in audio 4 mentioned being surrounded by kids. Where was he?
- [ ] At home with his brothers and friends.
- [ ] At the hospital, with pneumonia.

Post-listening

 Discuss these questions with your classmates.

a Do you have any childhood memory similar to the ones that were mentioned in the audio?

b In your opinion, what in your life could become a good memory in the future?

L3

Sync Speaking: My childhood

Pre-speaking

1 Choose a good childhood memory that you would like to share with your classmates. Then describe an object, a place, a sound, a smell, a drawing or anything that could represent this memory.

_____

_____

Speaking

2 Now you are going to talk to a partner about this good childhood memory and the representation that you have chosen. Follow the instructions.

a Think about what is important to mention when you describe your memory: when it happened or used to happen, where it happened, who you were with, the reason why it became a special memory etc.

b Write sentences about your memory.

c If possible, bring pictures of the chosen moment or place.

d Tell your partner about your childhood memory and what you have chosen to represent it.

> **Useful language**
>
> When I was a little child…
> When I was (7) years old…
> I used to (go to the beach with my family).
> I loved (games).
> I loved to (play with my brothers).
> I didn't like (seesaw).
> I didn't like to (play hide-and-seek).

Post-speaking

3 Read the questions and check the possible options.

a How did you feel when you shared your childhood memory with your partner?

☐ calm ☐ nervous ☐ shy
☐ happy ☐ sad ☐ other: _____

b How did the symbol you have chosen to represent the memory help you describe your story?

☐ It helped me remember details of my childhood memory.
☐ It helped my partner understand my memory.
☐ It helped me be calm during my conversation.
☐ Other: _____

4 Now share your childhood memory with the whole class. Was there any memory similar to the one you told?

_____

Studio Blog post

What: a blog post
To whom: for personal use; other students
Media: paper; digital
Objective: describe a childhood memory with someone special

1. Think of special moments from your childhood. Who used to be with you in them? Choose one picture of a special moment with this person.
2. Describe the picture. Take notes and organize them into topics.
3. Read the topics. Which ones should be mentioned in your blog post? Write sentences using connectors.
4. Share your text with a partner and ask for feedback. Give him/her some feedback too.
5. Revise your text.
6. Decide on the best layout to make your blog post more interesting.
7. Publish your work on the **Students for PEACE Social Media** <www.studentsforpeace.com.br>, using the tag **blogpost** or others chosen by the students.
8. Read your classmates' posts. Which memories are funny? Which ones are moving?

Peace talk

Chapters 7 and 8
Moral of the story

1 Discuss these questions with your classmates.

a Você se lembra de algum conto de fadas que tenha lido e do qual tenha gostado? Qual era a história?

b O que você sabe sobre o objetivo dos contos de fadas?

c Alguns contos de fadas apresentam histórias consideravelmente impressionantes ou até assustadoras. Em sua opinião, por que será que as pessoas criavam esse tipo de ficção justamente para crianças?

2 Which fairy tales do these pictures represent? Write their title.

a

b

c

3 Read the texts and match them to their corresponding pictures in activity 2.

Once there was a hardworking girl with a heart of gold and a wicked stepmother. She got a makeover from a fairy godmother and scored a dream date at the ball with a prince who tracked her down by her single lost glass slipper... And this story crossed the globe for thousands of years, winning hearts wherever it went.

☐ In a time of famine, a boy and a girl are abandoned in a great forest by their wicked stepmother. Unable to resist eating pieces of a real gingerbread cottage, the hungry children are captured by the cannibal witch who lives there; in the end, they must shove her into her own fiery oven to escape.

☐ A girl sets off alone to visit her grandmother with instructions not to step off the forest path—advice she promptly disregards, attracting the attention of a talking wolf who sets out to eat and impersonate Grandma. What happens next depends on what you read (because there are different versions).

Adapted from <https://www.rd.com/culture/most-popular-fairy-tale-stories/>. Accessed on May 31, 2019.

4 What can we learn from each fairy tale? Match each story to its possible moral.

a *Hansel and Gretel*

b *Little Red Riding Hood*

c *Cinderella*

☐ Deve-se sempre obedecer às recomendações dos pais ou dos/as responsáveis. Deve-se evitar fazer alguns trajetos desacompanhados/as.

☐ Nunca se deve deixar de sonhar, ainda que os sonhos pareçam impossíveis. Deve-se fazer o que é certo, ainda que as condições sejam adversas.

☐ Nunca se deve aceitar comida de estranhos. Nunca se deve entrar na casa de estranhos sem a companhia dos pais e/ou responsáveis. Deve-se sempre desconfiar de algo atraente demais que nos é oferecido gratuitamente.

5 Work on a campaign to help children avoid dangerous situations. Follow the instructions.

a Trabalhem em grupos. Façam um levantamento de outros contos de fadas e apontem quais são as possíveis lições que eles apresentam.

b Discutam quais ensinamentos das histórias pesquisadas são mais pertinentes nos dias de hoje. Façam uma lista dos perigos dos quais as crianças poderiam se proteger caso conhecessem essas histórias.

c Pesquisem quais são os maiores perigos para as crianças atualmente. Considerem a realidade de onde vocês moram.

d Escolham uma história entre as que foram tratadas até agora. Façam as adaptações necessárias a fim de apresentar uma moral da história (uma lição) que sirva de alerta para as crianças. Essas crianças podem ser estudantes mais jovens de sua escola, por exemplo.

e Montem um cartaz apresentando a história adaptada. Ilustrem o trabalho com recursos visuais que ajudem a comunicar a mensagem desejada. Escolham, com a ajuda do/a professor/a, o/s melhor/es lugar/es para dispor os cartazes da turma.

Self-assessment

Chapter 1 – Going online

Can you explore research and study tools?

Can you recognize vocabulary related to gadgets?

Can you understand the uses of the present simple?

Can you write tutorials?

Chapter 2 – Expression

Can you recognize different kinds of artistic expression?

Can you understand and use the modal verb "can" to describe abilities in the present?

Can you understand poems?

Can you write *haikus*?

Chapter 3 – Meet my culture

Can you discuss cultural differences?

Can you recognize vocabulary related to clothes and accessories?

Can you understand and use *wh-* words?

Can you understand interviews?

Chapter 4 – Food and nutrition

Can you distinguish between countable and uncountable nouns?

Can you read and create cooking recipes?

Can you understand and use adverbs of frequency to talk about eating habits?

Can you understand and use the imperative in recipe instructions?

Chapter 5 – Entertainment

Can you discuss different forms of entertainment?

Can you identify the use of prepositions of time?

Can you explore and create timelines?

Can you use the past simple to understand and create oral and written texts?

Chapter 6 – People and their stories

Can you explore and write biographies?

Can you identify the use of connectors that express addition, contrast, time, cause and consequence?

Can you reflect on the life stories of people who made a difference because of their contributions to important causes?

Can you understand and use the past simple of irregular verbs?

Chapter 7 – History is all around us

Can you explore and write encyclopedia entries?

Can you recognize different kinds of landmarks?

Can you understand and create oral narratives?

Can you understand and use the past continuous to describe events that were in progress at a certain time in the past?

Chapter 8 – When I was a kid

Can you explore and write blog posts?

Can you understand and share childhood memories?

Can you understand and use the modal verb "could" to describe abilities in the past?

Can you understand and use "used to" to talk about habits in the past?

Workbook

Name: _____ Class: _____ Date: _____

Chapter 1 — Going online

1 Read the text and check the appropriate options.

YOUNG PEOPLE PREFER PRINT TO E-BOOKS

Published September 30, 2015 by Charlotte Eyre

Print is still more popular than e-books among readers aged 16-24, although teenagers are more likely to read e-books than their older counterparts, according to the results of a survey carried out with 1,000 respondents aged 16-24 by Luke Mitchell for The Bookseller Children's Conference.

The 16-19s are less likely to have a preference for either print or e-books, with 23% of that group saying they are indifferent about format. Less than a fifth of the older group said they didn't have a preference.

The younger age group were also more likely to say they don't read any books (23%) than the older group (16%).

The majority (64%) said that less than £3 would be the right price for an e-book, whilst 26% said they would be willing to pay between £3 and £5.

One respondent said, "E-books should not cost the same as print books. Sometimes print books are cheaper than their electronic equivalents!"

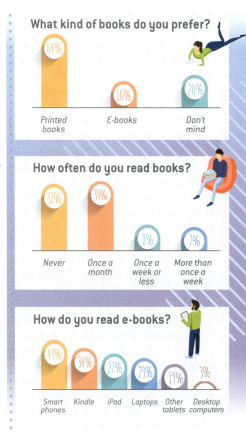

Adapted from <https://www.thebookseller.com/news/young-people-prefer-print-e-books-313321#>. Accessed on May 7, 2019.

a The number of young people who don't read any books is higher among...

☐ young adults.   ☐ teenagers.

b We can infer that this article was written in the United Kingdom because...

☐ the currency used is the pound sterling.   ☐ the currency used is the American dollar.

c One of the young people that participated in the survey complained about...

☐ the price of printed books.   ☐ the price of e-books.

2 Read the text in activity 1 again. Then write *T* (true) or *F* (false).

a ☐ The article uses only written text.
b ☐ There is only one type of graph in the article.
c ☐ Very few young people use their smartphones to read e-books.
d ☐ The majority of young people prefer printed books.
e ☐ Most young people seldom read any books.

3 Find the following information in the article.

a The name of the author: _____

b The date of publication: _____

c The name of the person who organized the survey: _____

4 Read the texts and complete them using the cues given in parentheses. Use the present simple.

a

Headphones and its risk of hearing loss

Headphones and earbuds are everywhere – but that _____ (not mean) they're safe for your ears. Using them can cause damage to your hearing if you are exposed to loud noise for too long.

Adapted from <https://www.audiorecovery.com/blog/do-headphones-increase-your-risk-hearing-loss>. Accessed on April 28, 2019.

c

What are drones?

Drones are aerial vehicles that _____ (not need) piloting. They have preprogrammed flight plans and fly in straight lines or circles. Many of them can hover in place as well.
Anyone can pilot a drone these days. While some drones _____ (have) military uses, others are used for aerial photography and other purposes.

Adapted from <https://quadcopterarena.com/15-little-known-facts-about-drones/>. Accessed on April 29, 2019.

b

Print vs. digital: Which is better for your eyesight?

The question is, how _____ each _____ (affect) our eyes? Computer screens, smartphones and tablets _____ (display) text and images differently than e-readers and print, using tiny pieces called "pixels". Focusing on pixels _____ (make) our eyes work a little harder than if we were reading a traditional book. The concern with printed books _____ (be) lighting. Reading in poor light _____ (make) it more difficult for the eyes to focus, thus causing eye fatigue. In the end, the take-home message is this: you should rest your eyes no matter what.

Adapted from <https://specialtyeye.com/2016/04/28/print-vs-digital-which-is-better-for-your-eyesight/>. Accessed on April 29, 2019.

Chapter 2 Expression

1 Read the poem and write *T* (true) or *F* (false).

UNDERFACE
Shel Silverstein

*Underneath my outside face
There's a face that none can see.
A little less smiley,
A little less sure,
But a whole lot more like me.*

Available at <https://www.commonlit.org/texts/underface>. Accessed on April 28, 2019.

a ☐ In the poem, the speaker expresses his real personality and emotions in public.
b ☐ In the poem, the speaker hides some of his emotions when he is in public.
c ☐ It is possible to assume that the speaker needs to show a more decided or happy face in some situations.
d ☐ According to the poem, both the outside face and the "underface" are similar.

2 Answer these questions.

a Do you have an underface? What do you think people don't know about you?
_____
_____

b Would you like people to see your underface? Why? How would you feel?
_____
_____

c In your opinion, does everybody show their real faces in public? Why?
_____
_____

3 Look at the pictures and match them to the sentences about these people's abilities.

☐ She can play the saxophone.
☐ They can do judo.
☐ She can sing and dance.
☐ She can paint.
☐ She can ride a horse.
☐ They can solve the Rubik's cube.

4 What about you? What can you do? What can't you do?

_____
_____
_____

Workbook

Name: _____ Class: _____ Date: _____

Chapter 3 — Meet my culture

1 Read the interview. Then write *T* (true) or *F* (false).

> **Want to be a foreign correspondent? She's got some heartfelt advice to offer**
>
> How has foreign correspondence changed over the years? I asked Aya Batrawy, an Associated Press correspondent based in Dubai.
>
> **Aya, what skills should you have before landing in a place like the AP in Dubai?**
> The first skill is the ability to be a good listener and to truly be open-minded when covering a different region, country, culture and society. Having strong writing skills to convey complex issues in an entertaining and informative way is also important to tell a story.
>
> **How do you maintain the energy to cover such a wide area and the critical thinking to prioritize?**
> To prioritize my time and energy, I try to avoid spending too much time on the stories that are being pushed by governments and their public relations firms. Instead, I try to follow the stories of anonymous people on Twitter, the stories of women who are fleeing abusive families.
>
> **Help me out. A story happens. What do you do?**
> The first thing that I do as a writer is confirm the news and write it. We then work together as a team – writers, video journalists and photographers.
>
> **Aya, thanks for the time, and good luck with the big stories coming up in your region.**
> Thank you.

Adapted from <https://www.poynter.org/reporting-editing/2018/want-to-be-a-foreign-correspondent-shes-got-some-heartfelt-advice-to-offer/>. Accessed on April 29, 2019.

a ☐ Aya Batrawy is a journalist who works as a foreign correspondent in Dubai.

b ☐ Journalists like Aya have to do all the work by themselves: write the story, take pictures and make videos.

c ☐ Aya prefers to follow the stories suggested by public relations firms instead of those of anonymous people.

d ☐ In her opinion, being able to write about complicated matters in an interesting way is an important ability.

e ☐ It is not necessary to confirm whether the story is true before writing and publishing it.

f ☐ Working as a correspondent, it's important to pay attention to what people say and be receptive to different ideas.

2 Complete the sentences with the appropriate object pronouns.

a If your friend wants to learn our language, we can teach _____ .

b Can you help _____ ? It's my first time abroad.

c What a rich culture! Please tell me more about _____ .

d Sabrina never forgets her parents when she travels. She always brings _____ a souvenir.

e We met a lot of nice people in Chile. They helped _____ whenever we needed something.

117

3 Match the questions about Leticia and Graham to the appropriate answers.

a **Where** does Leticia live now?
b **What** does she like about Mexico?
c **Why** is she living there?
d **Who** is with her in the picture?
e **When** does she go to the beach?

f **Where** are Graham and his family living?
g **How** does he feel about it?
h **When** did he move to this country?
i **Who** is his best friend in Brazil?
j **Why** did he move from his country?

☐ Because she wants to learn Spanish.
☐ Her friend Emilia.
☐ In Mexico.
☐ On the weekends.
☐ Its people, culture, language, music and beautiful beaches.

☐ In February.
☐ It's Larissa.
☐ In Brazil.
☐ Because his parents now work for a Brazilian company.
☐ Fine. Everybody is nice to him and he has some new friends.

4 Take a look at the clothes and accessories in the pictures. Then label them using the words in the box.

bracelet   cap   necklace   skirt   sneakers   sunglasses   tank top

a
b
c

Workbook

Name: _____ Class: _____ Date: _____

Chapter 4 Food and nutrition

1 Read the recipe and find the verbs in the imperative. Then write them.

Super Yummy Chocolate Chunk Oatmeal Cookies

★★★★★
90 Reviews

Level: **Easy** Prep: **15 min** Yield: **3 dozen cookies**
Total: **30 min** Cook: **15 min**

INGREDIENTS

- 2 cups flour
- 1 cup rolled oats
- 1 teaspoon baking powder
- ½ teaspoon cinnamon
- ½ teaspoon salt
- 1 cup brown sugar
- ½ cup granulated sugar
- 2 sticks unsalted butter, at room temperature
- 2 eggs
- Vanilla
- 12 ounces block dark chocolate, coarsely chopped
- 1 cup walnuts, chopped
- Large flake sea salt, for garnish

DIRECTIONS

1. Preheat the oven to 350 degrees F.
2. In a small bowl, combine the flour, oats, baking powder, cinnamon and salt.
3. In a large bowl, combine the brown sugar, granulated sugar and butter. Beat together the butter and sugar and add the eggs and the vanilla.
4. Gradually add the flour mixture into the butter/sugar mixture. Fold in the chocolate chunks and walnuts.
5. Spoon the cookie dough by 2 tablespoon-sized balls onto the ungreased cookie sheet. Place the cookie sheet in the oven and bake for 12 to 13 minutes.
6. When the cookies come out of the oven, IMMEDIATELY sprinkle each cookie with a few grains of sea salt.
7. Let the cookies cool for 2 to 3 minutes and then transfer them to a cooling rack.

Adapted from <https://www.foodnetwork.com/recipes/anne-burrell/super-yummy-chocolate-chunk-oatmeal-cookies-recipe-1925073>.
Accessed on April 30, 2019.

2 Look for the names of these ingredients in the recipe and write them below the corresponding pictures.

3 These verbs are frequently used in recipes. Match them to the pictures.

a pour   b stir   c peel   d chop

Workbook

Name: _____ Class: _____ Date: _____

Chapter 5 Entertainment

1 Read the timeline and complete the sentences with the past simple form of the verbs in parentheses.

EVOLUTION OF THE MOBILE PHONE

How _____ mobile phones _____ (get) to be this advanced?

1983-1990 | The First Ever Portable Mobile Phone

In 1983, the world _____ (gain) the first ever portable mobile phone in the shape of the Motorola DynaTAC 8000X. It cost US$4,000.
Feature from this era: Mobile calling.

1991-1994 | Dawn of Consumer Handsets

GSM first _____ (launch) in Europe in 1991, with the Orbitel TPU 900 first to market, but it wasn't until 1992 that mobiles were no longer restricted to business use.
Features from this era: SMS, games.

1995-1998 | A Splash of Color

Although it only _____ (offer) four colors, the Siemens S10 brought mobile phone displays to life for the first time in 1997.
Features from this era: E-mail, vibrate alerts, color screen.

1999-2002 | Growth of the Feature Phone

In 2000, Sharp _____ (introduce) the world's very first camera phone, the J-SH04.
Features from this era: WAP, Tri-Band, video calling, GPS navigation, predictive text, camera, polyphonic ringtones, MP3 player, Bluetooth, memory card, MMS.

2003-2006 | Mobile Data Revolution

With the advent of front-facing cameras in 2003, people _____ (start) video calling, although this technology _____ (not become) popular right away.
Features from this era: Realtone ringtones, augmented reality, Wi-Fi, Quad-Band, waterproof, full web browsing.

2007-2010 | Getting Smarter

Swiping and scrolling _____ (replace) the button method of input. The LG Prada _____ (present) the first touchscreen to market in May 2007, ahead of the Apple iPhone.
Features from this era: NFC, capacitive touchscreen, mobile apps, wireless charging.

2011-2014 | Life Companion

Smartphones became increasingly central to modern life, offering much more than just communication features. Voice recognition became common place first with Google Voice. Later, Apple _____ (launch) Siri into the market.
Features from this era: Voice control, dual-lens camera, facial recognition, fingerprint scanning, full HD screen, heart rate monitor.

2015-2018 | Size Matters

Screen sizes _____ (continue) to grow. Mobile payments also _____ (emerge), with Apple Pay and Android Pay offering users the possibility of shopping with their smartphones.
Features from this era: Iris scanner, Apple & Android Pay, Bezel less screen, Notch, in-display fingerprint sensor.

Adapted from <https://www.tigermobiles.com/evolution/#start>. Accessed on May 5, 2019.

2 Now write *T* (true) or *F* (false) according to the timeline in activity 1.
a ☐ Until the late 1990s, people used cell phones mostly for business purposes.
b ☐ The first cell phone with a colored screen had only four colors.
c ☐ The first mobile phone was expensive and could only make portable phone calls.
d ☐ Touchscreen technology started to be used in 2003.
e ☐ Cell phones gained front-facing cameras in 2000.

3 Complete the sentences using the past simple form of the verbs from the box. Then circle the appropriate prepositions used with them.

> end   extend   finish   increase   open   participate   receive   stop

a We _____ our presentation about augmented reality **in/on/at** 11:30 a.m.

b **In/On/At** June 2016, she _____ in a technology fair in Texas.

c The game _____ **in/on/at** Saturday **in/on/at** 10 a.m.

d Cell phone use _____ **in/on/at** the early 1990s and never _____ growing.

e She bought her virtual reality glasses online **in/on/at** April 15 and _____ them at home two days later.

f He _____ a comic bookstore **in/on/at** 2011 and _____ his business a few years later as more people became interested in this kind of entertainment.

4 Complete the questions using the past simple form of the verbs in parentheses. Then answer the questions.

a What toys or electronic devices _____ you _____ to play with when you were a small child? (like)
_____

b How _____ your parents _____ in their teenage years? (communicate)
_____

c What _____ you _____ the last time you went to the movies? (watch)
_____

Chapter 6 People and their stories

1 Read the text and complete it with the verbs from the box in the past simple.

be   have   lead   marry   organize   promote   rise   speak   stage

Martin Luther King, Jr.

Martin Luther King, Jr., original name Michael King, Jr., was born on January 15, 1929, in Atlanta, Georgia, U.S. He _____ the civil rights movement in the United States from the mid-1950s until his death in 1968. His leadership _____ fundamental to that movement's success in ending the legal segregation of African Americans in the South and in other parts of the United States. He was awarded the Nobel Peace Prize in 1964.

King _____ to national prominence as head of the Southern Christian Leadership Conference, which _____ nonviolent tactics, such as the famous March on Washington. He _____ and _____ a lot of marches and boycotts.

His most notable work is his "I Have a Dream" speech (1963), in which he _____ of his dream of living in a country that was free from segregation and racism.

In 1953, King _____ Coretta Scott, and together they _____ four children: Yolanda, Martin Luther III, Dexter Scott and Bernice.

Based on <https://www.britannica.com/biography/Martin-Luther-King-Jr#ref3915>. Accessed on May 7, 2019.

2 Complete the questions and answers about the life of Martin Luther King, Jr. Use the past simple of the verbs given.

a What _____ Martin Luther King, Jr. _____? (do)
He _____ for the end of racial segregation in the United States. (fight)

b What _____ his protests like? (be)
They _____ peaceful and organized. (be)

c How many kids _____ Luther King and Coretta Scott _____? (have)
They _____ four children: Yolanda, Martin Luther III, Dexter Scott and Bernice. (have)

d When _____ he _____? (die)
He _____ in 1968. (die)

123

3 Read the text about Gertrude Ederle and circle the appropriate connectors. Then complete it with the past simple form of the verbs in parentheses.

The first woman to swim the English Channel

"England or drown!" proclaimed the New York Daily News. It _____ (be) August 6, 1926, the day that Gertrude Ederle _____ (become) the first woman to swim the English Channel.

Only five men had ever swum the waterway before. The challenges included quickly changing tides, six-foot waves, frigid temperatures **and/because/after** lots of jellyfish.

Ederle was born in October 1905 in New York City. She joined the Women's Swimming Association **so/and/but** _____ (win) her first local competition award at age 16.

She first tried to cross the English Channel in 1925, **and/but/so** _____ (not make) it all the way across. The British press claimed she was disqualified **before/but/because** someone in the support boat had touched her (support boat riders could give her food and drink, but couldn't touch her). However, Gavin Mortimer, author of *The Great Swim*, says the British press invented this story out of a sense of national rivalry.

The next year, she _____ (wear) a lighter two-piece bathing suit and was better prepared. She not only arrived at the French end of the channel, but also _____ (beat) the previous men's times – swimming 35 miles in 14 and a half hours.

Ederle's achievement _____ (make) a lasting contribution to women's sports and paved the way for other female swimmers. The next four people to successfully swim the channel after her _____ (be) all women.

Adapted from <https://www.history.com/news/gertrude-ederle-first-woman-swim-english-channel>. Accessed on May 16, 2019.

Workbook

Chapter 7 — History is all around us

1 Read the text about Notre-Dame de Paris. Then write T (true) or F (false).

Notre-Dame de Paris, also called **Notre-Dame Cathedral**, is a cathedral in Paris. It is the most famous of all the Gothic cathedrals of the Middle Ages and is distinguished for its size, antiquity and architectural interest.

The cathedral was initiated by Maurice de Sully, bishop of Paris, who, around year 1160, had the idea of converting the ruins of the two earlier basilicas into a single building, on a larger scale. The foundation stone was laid by Pope Alexander III in 1163, and the high altar was consecrated in 1189. The choir, the western facade and the nave were completed by 1250, and porches, chapels and other embellishments were added over the next 100 years.

Notre-Dame Cathedral suffered damage and deterioration through the centuries. After the French Revolution, it was rescued from possible destruction by Napoleon, who crowned himself emperor of the French in the cathedral in 1804. Notre-Dame underwent major restorations by French architect Eugène-Emmanuel Viollet-le-Duc in the mid-19th century. The popularity of Victor Hugo's historical novel *Notre-Dame de Paris* (1831), whose story is set in the cathedral, was said to have inspired the renovations. During a restoration campaign in 2019, a fire broke out in the cathedral's attic, and the massive blaze destroyed most of the roof, Viollet-le-Duc's 19th-century spire and some of the rib vaulting.

Adapted from <https://www.britannica.com/topic/Notre-Dame-de-Paris>. Accessed on May 7, 2019.

a ☐ Notre-Dame Cathedral's construction began in 1163.

b ☐ Notre-Dame had never been damaged until the fire in 2019.

c ☐ The construction of the cathedral was finished in few years.

d ☐ People believe the restauration of the cathedral in the mid-19th century inspired Victor Hugo's novel.

2 Read the sentences and circle the appropriate form of the verbs.

a We **looked/were looking** at the photos we took at Notre-Dame when we **heard/were hearing** about the fire on TV.

b When I **entered/was entering** the National History Museum, a few students **watched/were watching** a video about World War II.

c Which landmarks **did they restore/were they restoring** when she **arrived/was arriving** at the city?

d I **read/was reading** a book about the early post-war years when the library lights **went/were going** out.

3 Take a look at these historic pictures. Then complete their descriptions using the past continuous form of the verbs from the box.

> destroy   hold   say   sit

The Germans _____ the Berlin wall, which divided the country from 1961 to 1989.

A soldier _____ goodbye to his wife before leaving for World War I, in 1917.

A black woman _____ in a wagon reserved for white people. She did that as a protest during apartheid in South Africa, in 1952.

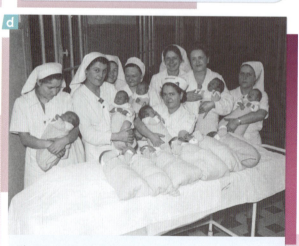

The nurses _____ newborns at a hospital in Paris.

Workbook

Name: _____ Class: _____ Date: _____

Chapter 8 — When I was a kid

1 Read the texts and match them to the pictures.

Kids these days: A portrait of childhood around the world

a In Amsterdam at 3:00 p.m., Benjamin, 9, is going for an impromptu swim with friends in the River Ij. There's no anxiety from his father. "He has his swimming diploma and he knows he needs to stay away from shipping".

b China's school system remains one of the most pressurized in the world. Students start the day at 7:00 a.m. and finish at 8:30 p.m., after three hours of supervised homework. Jianhong, 10, admits taking out his cell phone during some lessons.

c Abdulatef, 11, lives in Saudi Arabia and likes playing computer games and going for camel rides on the beach. He plays football on a field overlooked by a huge model of the Koran.

d Most British children know which brands are which, and the internet permeates almost every aspect of their childhood. Toys have become status symbols. Lewis, 10, for example, bought a pack of toys for £10 and sold it online for £1,000 after finding an ultra-rare.

Adapted from <https://www.telegraph.co.uk/news/worldnews/10317562/Kids-these-days-A-portrait-of-childhood-around-the-world.html>. Accessed on May 8, 2019.

2 Imagine that the children mentioned in activity **1** are now adults. Then write sentences about them. Use the verb form *used to*.

_____
_____
_____
_____

3 Complete the texts with the past simple or the past continuous form of the verbs in parentheses. Then circle a verb that expresses ability in the past.

a
When I was little and my parents _____ (buy) mushrooms to cook, I always _____ (take) one out of the package and _____ (keep) it as a pet for the day. At night, my parents would take it out of the little bed I had made for it and put it back in the fridge. I always assumed it _____ (go) back to the forest.

b
Today, a little girl _____ (need) O- blood. We _____ (not have) any at the hospital, but her brother could donate some to her. He _____ (sit) quietly and then _____ (say) goodbye to his parents. After we took his blood, he asked, "When will I die?" He _____ (think) he _____ (give) his life for hers. Thankfully, they both were fine.

c
So, I _____ (buy) school supplies for my students, when this man _____ (start) asking me questions like "Why are you buying 150 notebooks?". I _____ (explain) that I teach Science and that it _____ (not be) worth the hassle of trying to get kids to bring their own notebooks, and that it takes time away from classes. He then _____ (proceed) to pay for my entire cart of supplies. His son _____ (watch) the whole thing. There are some really good people in this world.

4 Complete the sentences with the past simple or the past continuous form of the verbs in parentheses.

a My little brother _____ (not want) to go to school this morning because it _____ (rain).

b My cousin and I _____ (want) to invite Lizz for a sleepover, but she _____ (not go) to school yesterday. She _____ (have) an audition.

c I _____ (call) Lucas last night, but he _____ (not can) talk to me. He _____ (study) for his test.

d When Mary _____ (enter) the classroom last Friday, everybody _____ (stop) talking. They _____ (plan) a surprise party for her.

Irregular verbs list

Infinitive	Past simple	Past participle	Translation
be	was/were	been	*estar; ser*
become	became	become	*tornar(-se)*
bring	brought	brought	*trazer*
build	built	built	*construir*
catch	caught	caught	*pegar*
cut	cut	cut	*cortar*
do	did	done	*fazer*
drink	drank	drunk	*beber*
fall	fell	fallen	*cair*
feel	felt	felt	*sentir*
find	found	found	*achar, encontrar*
forbid	forbade	forbidden	*proibir*
forget	forgot	forgotten	*esquecer*
get	got	got/gotten	*chegar; ficar; obter*
give	gave	given	*dar*
go	went	gone	*ir*
have	had	had	*ter*
hide	hid	hidden	*esconder, ocultar*
keep	kept	kept	*guardar; manter*
know	knew	known	*conhecer; saber*
leave	left	left	*deixar; partir*
let	let	let	*deixar, permitir*
lose	lost	lost	*perder*
make	made	made	*fazer; preparar*
meet	met	met	*encontrar(-se)*
overcome	overcame	overcome	*superar; vencer*
put	put	put	*por; colocar*
ride	rode	ridden	*andar (a cavalo, de bicicleta, de moto etc.)*
run	ran	run	*correr*
say	said	said	*dizer*
see	saw	seen	*ver*
send	sent	sent	*enviar*
speak	spoke	spoken	*falar*
spend	spent	spent	*gastar*
take	took	taken	*aceitar; levar; pegar; tomar*
teach	taught	taught	*ensinar*
tell	told	told	*contar, dizer*
think	thought	thought	*achar; pensar*
throw	threw	thrown	*atirar, lançar*
wake up	woke up	woken up	*acordar, despertar*
wear	wore	worn	*vestir, usar*
write	wrote	written	*escrever*

Language reference

Chapter 1 — Present simple (review)

Usa-se o *present simple* para expressar:

- uma informação no presente:
  *My friends **live** in Madrid.*

- uma rotina ou um hábito:
  *We **have** French classes on Tuesdays and Thursdays.*

- um fato ou uma verdade universal:
  *Water **freezes** at zero degrees Celsius.*

O *present simple* é formado pela forma básica do verbo sem *to*:

*I **live** in Manaus.*

*You **play** tennis very well.*

*They **like** music.*

Na 3ª pessoa do singular (*he*, *she*, *it*) acrescenta-se *-s* ao verbo:

*He **lives** in Cape Town.*

*She **plays** soccer very well.*

*It **rains** a lot in Belém.*

Como exceções, na 3ª pessoa do singular:

- acrescenta-se *-es* aos verbos terminados em *ss*, *sh*, *ch*, *x*, *z* e *o*:
  to kiss – kisses
  to wash – washes
  to watch – watches
  to fix – fixes
  to buzz – buzzes
  to go – goes

- substitui-se *y* por *-ies* em verbos terminados em *y* e precedidos de consoante:
  to study – studies
  to try – tries

- o verbo *to have* é irregular e tem a forma *has*.

As formas negativa e interrogativa do *present simple* apresentam-se da seguinte maneira:

Negative	
I study French.	I **don't study** French.
She goes to school in the morning.	She **doesn't go** to school in the morning.

Interrogative	
You play tennis.	**Do** you **play** tennis?
He likes music.	**Does** he **like** music?

Chapter 2 — "Can"/"Can't"

O verbo modal *can* é usado para:

- expressar habilidade/capacidade:
  Look! The baby **can** walk.

- pedir permissão:
  Can I use your pencil?

- expressar uma possibilidade:
  It **can** rain this afternoon.

Affirmative	Negative	Interrogative	Short answers
I **can** write poems.	He **cannot** sing. He **can't** sing.	**Can** she swim?	Yes, she **can**. No, she **can't**.

Chapter 3 — Wh- words, subject and object pronouns

As *wh- words* são usadas da seguinte forma:

- para perguntar "o que", usa-se "*what*":
  What is he doing now?

- para perguntar "onde", usa-se "*where*":
  Where is the library?

- para perguntar "quando", usa-se "*when*":
  When is your birthday?

- para perguntar "por que", usa-se "*why*":
  Why are you tired?

- para perguntar "quem", usa-se "*who*":
  Who is your Math teacher?

- para perguntar "como", usa-se "*how*":
  How can I make a kite?

Os *subject pronouns* são usados como sujeitos de verbos e os *object pronouns* são usados como objetos de verbos, portanto estes normalmente aparecem após um verbo ou uma preposição.

Subject pronouns	Object pronouns
I	me
you	you
he	him
she	her
it	it
we	us
you	you
they	them

Chapter 4 — Imperative

Usa-se o *imperative* para expressar:

- uma instrução ou um comando:
  Make a list of the ingredients you need.

- uma sugestão ou um conselho:
  Put on your coat. It's cold outside.

O *imperative* é constituído pela forma básica do verbo e sua forma negativa usa o auxiliar *do not* (*don't*):

Affirmative	Negative
Open the door.	**Don't open** the door.

Chapter 5 — Past simple of regular verbs

O *past simple* é usado para referir-se a eventos que ocorreram em um período determinado do passado.

Forma-se o *past simple* acrescentando *-ed* ao final dos verbos regulares, e a forma é a mesma para todos os pronomes:

to play – played

to wash – washed

Como exceções, existem estes casos:

- se o verbo terminar em *e*, acrescenta-se apenas *-d*:
  to like – liked
  to use – used

- se o verbo terminar em *y* e for precedido de consoante, substitui-se o *y* por *i* e acrescenta-se *-ed*.
  to study – studied
  to try – tried

- se o verbo tiver apenas uma sílaba ou terminar em vogal + consoante e a sílaba tônica for a última, duplica-se a consoante final e acrescenta-se *-ed*.
  to stop – stopped
  to permit – permitted

Affirmative	Negative	Interrogative	Short answers
She **studied**.	She **didn't study**.	**Did** she **study**?	Yes, she **did**. No, she **didn't**.

Chapter 6 — Past simple of irregular verbs

Os verbos irregulares possuem uma forma diferente. Não se acrescenta *-ed* para formar o *past simple* desses verbos:

to go – went

to see – saw

A forma do verbo é a mesma para todos os pronomes:

*I **went** to the movies yesterday.*

*She **went** to the movies on Monday.*

Affirmative	Negative	Interrogative	Short answers
He **saw** Mary this morning.	He **didn't see** Mary this morning.	**Did** he **see** Mary this morning?	Yes, he **did**. No, he **didn't**.

Chapter 7 — Past continuous

Usa-se o *past continuous* para referir-se a eventos que estavam em progresso em um período do passado.

O *past continuous* é formado pelo verbo auxiliar *to be* no passado + verbo principal no gerúndio (*-ing*):

Affirmative	Negative	Interrogative
They **were studying**.	They **weren't studying**.	**Were** they **studying**?

O *past continuous* pode ser usado com:

- *while* para expressar duas ações que estavam ocorrendo simultaneamente:
  *He **was studying** while his sister **was playing** the guitar.*

- *when* para expressar uma ação que estava acontecendo quando ocorreu outra:
  *He **was studying** when I **arrived**.*

Chapter 8 — Past simple, past continuous and "could"

O *past simple* refere-se a eventos que começaram e terminaram em um determinado momento do passado.

O *past continuous* refere-se a eventos que estavam em progresso em algum momento do passado.

O verbo modal *could* é utilizado, entre outras situações, para falar sobre habilidades do passado:

Affirmative	Negative	Interrogative	Short answers
I **could** play the guitar.	He **could not** dance. He **couldn't** dance.	**Could** she sing?	Yes, she **could**. No, she **couldn't**.

Interdisciplinary project
World Englishes

Presentation

Vamos conhecer um pouco sobre as variações linguísticas da língua inglesa por meio da música?

Procedures

Part I (English, Geography and History)

Objective: find artists who sing in English although it's not their native or first language.
Resources: internet and atlas (physical or digital).

Instructions

a. Pesquisem cantores/cantoras (artistas solo ou vocalistas de bandas) que cantem músicas em inglês apesar de esta não ser sua língua nativa. Considerem qualquer estilo musical. Selecionem artistas oriundos/as dos cinco continentes (África, América, Ásia, Europa e Oceania).

b. Agrupem todos/as os/as artistas selecionados/as de acordo com suas origens. O/A professor/a montará no quadro uma tabela com cinco colunas, uma para cada continente. Façam a distribuição dos nomes na tabela e, ao lado de cada nome, incluam o país de origem de cada artista.

c. A turma será organizada em cinco grupos, e a cada grupo serão atribuídos/as alguns/algumas dos/as artistas anotados/as no quadro.

d. Sob a orientação do/a professor/a de Geografia, pesquisem qual/quais é/são o/s idioma/s falado/s no país dos/as artistas atribuídos/as a seu grupo. Lembrem-se de que o fato de o inglês ser uma das línguas oficiais de um país não significa que ele seja a língua nativa de toda a população.

e. Pesquisem dados relacionados à qualidade de vida dos/as cidadãos/cidadãs desses países.

f. Com a orientação do/a professor/a de História, pesquisem quais idiomas mais influenciaram a cultura do/s país/es dos/as artistas com os/as quais seu grupo está trabalhando. Há alguma informação relevante descoberta nessa pesquisa?

g. Novamente, com a orientação de seu/sua professor/a de Geografia, elaborem um mapa destacando o/s país/es dos/as artistas atribuídos/as a seu grupo. Caso tenham dupla nacionalidade, destaquem ambos os países.

Analysis

Analisem os mapas elaborados e os idiomas falados nos países pesquisados. Há algum continente que tenha se destacado pela quantidade de artistas que cantam em língua inglesa? É possível observar se há algum elemento relacionado a esses/essas artistas que os/as vinculam a seus idiomas nativos? (Por exemplo, o nome artístico, o nome da sua banda, a recorrência de palavras da língua nativa nas letras de suas canções em inglês etc.) Há alguma relação aparente entre a opção por cantar em inglês e os dados encontrados sobre a qualidade de vida em seu país de origem? Comentem. Se necessário, peçam ajuda a seu/sua professor/a de História.

Reflections

Na opinião do grupo, que razões teriam levado esses/essas artistas a cantar (também ou apenas) em inglês? Quais devem ter sido (ou são) seus objetivos? Registrem suas ideias.

Part II (Math and Portuguese)

Objective: observe in which language the singers sing most of their songs.
Resources: internet, CDs, DVDs, music apps, bilingual dictionary and calculator.

Instructions

a. Com seu grupo, explorem a discografia dos/as artistas que estão sendo estudados/as. Pesquisem: de todos os álbuns lançados por esses/essas artistas, quantas músicas são cantadas em inglês? Quantas músicas são cantadas em seus idiomas nativos? Esses/Essas artistas cantam em outro idioma além do inglês e da sua língua nativa? Procurem descobrir: esses/essas artistas sempre cantaram em inglês ou decidiram fazê-lo a partir de um momento específico? Quando esses/essas artistas obtiveram maior repercussão na mídia e êxito profissional? É possível associar esses resultados ao fato de cantarem ou terem passado a cantar em inglês? Anotem todas as ideias.

b. Elaborem um gráfico representando a proporção entre as músicas que são cantadas em inglês e aquelas que são cantadas no idioma nativo desses/dessas artistas – e, se for o caso, em outros idiomas.

c. Busquem imagens dos/as artistas atribuídos/as a seu grupo, desde o início de suas carreiras até os dias atuais. Houve alguma alteração em seus estilos musicais ao longo dos anos? As músicas que cantam em inglês são, em geral, do mesmo gênero musical das que cantavam no seu idioma nativo ou em outras línguas? Selecionem imagens que possam representar possíveis mudanças de estilo/gênero. É possível, com base nos títulos das músicas, observar alguma mudança na trajetória musical desses/dessas artistas? Se necessário, consultem um dicionário bilíngue.

Analysis

Analisem os dados obtidos por seu grupo e procurem apontar vantagens e desvantagens relacionadas à opção desses/dessas artistas por cantar em língua inglesa em vez de seu idioma nativo. Quanto ao estilo musical inicial, ele se manteve ou esses/essas artistas parecem ter feito alterações? Procurem dados que possam embasar as respostas.

Reflections

1. Essa pesquisa, na opinião do grupo, ajudou a responder aos questionamentos do item "Reflections" da "Part I" do projeto? Se sim, de que forma?
2. É possível atribuir o uso da língua inglesa a uma maior abrangência da obra dos/as artistas estudados/as?
3. Na opinião do seu grupo, de que forma o idioma nativo desses/dessas artistas lhes conferia um estilo pessoal e único?
4. Quais vantagens a língua inglesa aparentemente trouxe para a carreira de cada artista pesquisado/a?
5. Algum outro dado chamou a atenção do grupo? Expliquem.

Part III (English and Art)

Objective: look for accents and different pronunciations.
Resources: internet, books and music videos.

Instructions

a. Com seu/sua professor/a de Língua Inglesa, ouçam músicas dos/as artistas que estão sendo pesquisados/as. Concentrem-se na pronúncia do idioma. É possível verificar se o idioma nativo desses/dessas artistas influenciou o modo como falam/cantam em inglês? O que mais chamou a atenção do grupo?

b. Pesquisem músicas e videoclipes desses/dessas artistas e observem se fazem alguma menção à sua cultura de origem. Em caso afirmativo, é possível observar se seu país de origem é representado com algum tipo de estereótipo?

Analysis

Analisem os dados coletados pelo grupo e respondam: 1. Que detalhes chamaram mais a sua atenção nos videoclipes desses/dessas artistas? 2. Como seus países de origem são representados em seus vídeos ou álbuns? 3. Esses/Essas artistas demonstram explorar suas origens ao longo de sua carreira ou isso não é feito com muita frequência? 4. Na opinião do grupo, por que isso acontece?

Justifiquem. Esses/Essas artistas alguma vez cantaram músicas de outros/as cantores/cantoras falantes de língua inglesa? Se sim, selecionem as duas versões e comparem o estilo e a pronúncia em uma e em outra situação. É possível notar diferenças?

c Busquem trechos de entrevistas concedidas em inglês por esses/essas artistas. Há alguma entrevista em que comentem sua experiência com o inglês ou sua adaptação à experiência de cantar em outro idioma?

d Selecionem os trechos mais representativos dos videoclipes, das músicas e das entrevistas e elaborem um roteiro para seu grupo fazer uma apresentação sobre os/as artistas. Escolham os detalhes que poderão enriquecer a discussão e embasar as ideias do grupo.

e Selecionem outras informações coletadas pelo grupo durante as pesquisas e decidam quais detalhes deverão ser mencionados na apresentação do grupo.

Reflections

1. O grupo considera que a pronúncia desses/dessas artistas em inglês sofre influência de seus idiomas nativos? Se sim, de que forma? 2. Na opinião do grupo, é possível notar tentativas desses/dessas artistas de esconder ou amenizar o próprio sotaque quando cantam em língua inglesa? 3. Esses/Essas artistas demonstram aproveitar suas origens e enfatizar seus sotaques característicos? 4. Esses/Essas artistas sofrem algum tipo de preconceito por conta de sua origem? Se sim, da parte de quem?

Sharing knowledge

Que tal criar um vídeo para os/as colegas de sua escola e, desse modo, apresentar as descobertas feitas ao longo do projeto?

Instructions

a Apresentem as questões e respostas da seção "Reflections" de todas as etapas aos/às professores/professoras que estão participando do projeto. Peçam-lhes que avaliem se as conclusões a que seu grupo chegou podem ser validadas ou se devem ser aprofundadas e modificadas.

b Com base nos apontamentos feitos por seus/suas professores/professoras, criem e editem um vídeo apresentando os trechos dos vídeos selecionados por seu grupo. Adicionem informações relevantes, como o idioma nativo dos/as artistas, seu país de origem, dados sobre suas carreiras e trajetórias, além de outras informações que o grupo julgar pertinentes. Na impossibilidade de criar um vídeo, selecionem imagens, canções e outros detalhes que possam enriquecer o trabalho, que pode ser feito por meio de cartazes e áudio.

Presentation

Com a supervisão de seu/sua professor/a de Língua Inglesa e dos/as professores/professoras das demais disciplinas que contribuíram para a elaboração das pesquisas e do projeto ao longo do ano, apresentem seus vídeos (ou cartazes) e suas análises.

Assessment

Avaliem, em conjunto com os/as professores/professoras envolvidos/as, os resultados obtidos com base em todas as pesquisas e discussões realizadas durante o projeto. Debatam, ainda, sobre como foi o processo de pesquisa em grupo e quais foram os ganhos e os desafios de realizar o trabalho em conjunto. Avaliem se os resultados alcançados correspondem ao que era esperado e discutam se há alguma possibilidade de aprofundar a pesquisa feita pelos grupos.

Transcripts

Chapter 1

Track 2 – Page 17

I belong to Gen Z, a generation born with complete technology. We have PCs, smartphones, gaming devices, tablets, MP3 players and the internet. We naturally multitask. We text, read, watch and walk at the same time, a skill that stuns the adults. We like to express our feelings and thoughts and share them with the world.

Track 3 – Page 17

In our lifetime, we'll not send a single letter by mail. But we'll spend at least 20% of our time on social media. Having too many gadgets also has a bad impact. We'd rather stay indoors and use our gadgets than play outdoors and be active.

Extracts from the audio available at <https://www.youtube.com/watch?v=qypKjzUOhBM>. Accessed on March 11, 2019.

Track 4 – Page 18

Interviewee 1: I use it for entertainment, for communication and just for finding out about anything that I think about.

Interviewee 2: Yeah, news, information, yeah, any… just general interesting things.

Interviewee 3: It's probably 90% just to connect with friends and then other stuff is for groups. Like, a lot of people have the internet, so you can get a message across to a wide variety of people.

Extracts from the audio available at <https://www.youtube.com/watch?v=l1FAJyHK5b0>. Accessed on March 11, 2019.

Chapter 2

Track 5: Parts 1, 2 and 3 (Track 6: Part 1; Track 7: Part 2; Track 8: Part 3) – Pages 28 and 29

Part 1

Hey, Black Child / Do you know who you are / Who you really are / Do you know you can be / What you want to be / If you try to be / What you can be

Part 2

Hey, Black Child / Do you know where you're going / Where you're really going / Do you know you can learn / What you want to learn / If you try to learn / What you can learn

Part 3

Hey, Black Child / Do you know you are strong / I mean really strong / Do you know you can do / What you want to do / If you try to do / What you can do

Hey, Black Child / Be what you can be / Learn what you must learn / Do what you can do / And tomorrow your nation / Will be what you want it to be

Extracts from the audio available at <https://www.youtube.com/watch?v=LIQbhj1ZiJk>. Accessed on March 19, 2019.

Chapter 3

Track 9 – Page 43

1: A powwow is a celebration of life. We all come together as one nation. And this is where they talk about the circle that we come in. This is where we meet friends. This is where we meet relatives. This is where we bring our children to, in a circle… they call it the circle of life.

2: When we look at the grand entry, it's a teaching right there. We have these flags that come in, the eagle staffs… and those represent nations, the families, communities […] And then we have the elders, then we've got the adults and then we have the children. The children have role models all the way down the line.

3: Without the beat of the drum, which is our heart, we would not have a powwow. So it is important that we respect and honor those people that come together to sit around the drum and make a circle.

Extracts from the audio available at <https://www.youtube.com/watch?v=Fv6DZTNkY5w>. Accessed on March 27, 2019.

Chapter 4

Track 10 – Page 55

Check the ten steps to a balanced and healthy eating plan.

One: make fresh food the starting point of your eating habits. This is the golden rule. Fresh ingredients are more balanced and have more nutrients.

Two: use oils, fat, salt and sugar moderately. These ingredients, in small quantities, add flavor to your food without harming its nutritious balance.

Three: limit the consumption of processed food. Use it only as part of a meal based on fresh ingredients. […]

Extracts from the audio available at <https://www.youtube.com/watch?v=JTk8NxESCUY>. Accessed on April 4, 2019.

Track 13 – Page 68

Announcer: OK! So in this episode, you are actually not reacting to a video.

Everhet: Alright.

Adam: Again. Fantastic.

Announcer: For you today, instead, we have this.

Alix: What is this?

Will: Ohhh, this is cool.

Reina: Oh! It's a game from, like, way back.

Jeordy: One side is baseball, one side is football!

Jeannie: B.O.

Thomas: B.O. Jackson Baseball.

Labib: Oh! Bo Jackson. I've heard the name.

Announcer: Any idea who Bo Jackson is?

Darius: Never heard of him.

Jeordy: No, I don't.

Alix: I don't know.

Sam: I'm assuming he plays football and baseball.

Announcer: In the early 90's, there was a company named Tiger Electric that made a bunch of these handheld games, just like that. And today you are going to experience playing a few of these old popular games.

Alix: Awesome! I'm excited.

Track 15 – Page 69

Announcer: So this game was a two-in-one, but we are just gonna have you play Bo Jackson Football.

Jeordy: This is gonna be interesting. I don't know how to play either of these sports.

Extracts from the audio available at <https://www.dailymotion.com/video/x5tyqrv>. Accessed on April 11, 2019.

Chapter 6

Track 17: Parts 1 and 2 (Track 18: Part 1) – Page 81

Part 1

Anne Frank was born on June 12th, 1929, in the city of Frankfurt, Germany. Twelve days later, little baby Anne and her mother, Edith, came home from the hospital. The Franks were like many other families of the time. Anne's father, Otto, was a businessman. Her mother stayed at home caring for Anne and Anne's older sister, Margot. The Franks led a comfortable life. There was a nanny to help Mrs. Frank. The family had nice clothes and good food. Anne had her own little sandbox to play in. Their apartment in Frankfurt was full of books.

Part 2

Otto was tall and thin; Edith was plump. Otto loved being around people. He was high-spirited and outgoing. Edith was shy and quiet. Otto loved to read to his daughters. He also made up wonderful stories at bedtime. Some were about two sisters named Paula. One of the Paulas was very well-behaved and polite, like Margot. The other Paula was always getting into lots of trouble. That Paula was more like Anne, who was full of mischief. Her father understood her. He and Anne were very much alike. Anne did not get along nearly as well with her mother. They often had fights. Anne was jealous because she felt that her sister was her mother's pet. While Margot was serious and mild-mannered, Anne was moody and had a temper. But she was also lively and full of fun. Both sisters had dark shining hair, large eyes and lovely smiles.

ABRAMSON, Ann. *Who Was Anne Frank?* Penguin Group USA and Audible, 2009.

Track 19 – Page 95

Hi, my name is Anna and this is my great-great-great-grandfather, Captain John Egge. He came to Australia from China in 1852 and worked as a cabin boy on board boats along the Murray River. He eventually got his own paddle steamer and was heavily involved in the river trade. He started up a heap of businesses in a town called Wentworth, in New South Wales, and became one of the wealthiest men there. It would've been pretty hard for him starting a new life, moving to a foreign country and learning a new language. But that was the case for many Chinese people who came to Australia around the same time. During the 1850s, tens of thousands of Chinese immigrants traveled here by boat. They came to work in Victoria's goldfields so they could make money to send back to their families. After the gold rush, many people went back to China, others stayed to start up their own businesses or to work the land. And today, there are around 865,000 people of Chinese background living in Australia, sharing their culture and talents with all of us. [...]

Chinese immigrants like my great-great-great-grandfather have played a big role in Australia's history. They've made our society more multicultural and brought their traditions to our country to enjoy. I reckon Captain John Egge would have been quite proud.

Extracts from the audio available at <http://education.abc.net.au/home#!/media/1957515/chinese-migration>. Accessed on May 10, 2019.

Track 20 — Page 107

1: I still remember when I learned my first magic trick! I was nine or ten years old. It was a very nice and mysterious trick! I performed it for my family and my friends. Everybody laughed at it!

2: I always loved spending time with my grandmother. She had other seven grandchildren, but she spent more time with me. She told me stories about the time when she was a child and about her mother and father.

3: When I was at school, I broke both my arms by falling off a swing! But, you know, bad things sometimes turn out to be great. I made many friends because of that! Everybody at school wanted to sign my plaster cast. I ended up talking to every kid at school!

4: I remember some things from when I was a child. Things were different. Oh, boy! That was many, many years ago. There was less traffic in the street and kids used to run around. I also remember that I got sick when I was six years old. I had to spend some days at a children's hospital 'cause I had pneumonia. There were lots of kids there.

Glossary

CHAPTER 1

A
according to: de acordo com
after: após
always: sempre
attend: frequentar

B
before: antes de
born: nascido/a
breakfast: café da manhã
buy: comprar

C
college: faculdade
current: atual

D
device: aparelho

E
evaluate: avaliar
even: até mesmo
excerpt: trecho

F
feeling: sentimento
file: arquivo
flash drive: *pen drive* (anglicismo)

G
gadget: dispositivo eletrônico
gather: reunir

H
have fun: divertir-se

I
interviewee: entrevistado/a

K
key: chave
keyboard: teclado
knowledge: conhecimento

L
letter: carta

M
make-up: maquiagem
match: associar
multitask: executar mais de uma tarefa ao mesmo tempo

N
no-brainer (informal): algo muito fácil
novelty: inovação, novidade

P
paper: trabalho escolar; papel
paste: colar
plagiarism: plágio

R
relate: relacionar-se
reliable: confiável
research: pesquisar; pesquisa

S
set up: montar
smart: (de forma) inteligente
sometimes: às vezes
sort: dividir, separar
source: fonte
speakers: autofalantes
statement: afirmação
step: passo
straight: direto/a
switch off: desligar

T
tool: ferramenta
transcript: transcrição

V
virtual reality headset: óculos de realidade virtual

W
without: sem

CHAPTER 2

A
acting: atuar; atuação
appreciate: valorizar

B
be able to: ser capaz de
benefit: beneficiar-se
bookworm: traça; rato de biblioteca (gíria)
borrow: pegar emprestado
brave: corajoso/a

C
challenge: desafio

D
dare: ousar
doubt: duvidar

E
effort: esforço
everyone: todo mundo

F
fire: fogo

G
gentle: gentil
get to know: conhecer
ground: chão

H
hat: chapéu

J
job: trabalho

K
kid: criança

L
liar: mentiroso/a
look like: parecer-se com

M
mob: multidão

N
need: precisar
notice: perceber
nourish: alimentar, nutrir; alentar, encorajar

O
order: encomenda; ordem

P
pass a law: aprovar uma lei
playwright: dramaturgo/a
politician: político/a

R
request: pedido

S
sad: triste
shed: desfolhar
shirt: camisa
somewhere: em algum lugar
song: música
stanza: estrofe
star: estrela
strength: força
sun: sol

T
theme: tema
travel: viajar
treat: tratar

U
unexpected: inesperado/a
unique: excepcional, único/a

W
war: guerra
wind: vento

CHAPTER 3

B
beat: batida
behind: atrás, por trás
belief: crença

C
cap: boné
care: importar-se
choice: escolha
clothing: roupa, vestimenta

D
desk: mesa de trabalho
dress: vestir-se; vestido
drum: tambor

E
eagle: águia
employer: empregador/a
exchange student: estudante intercambista

F
friendlier: mais simpático/a

G
giant: gigante
grow: cultivar, produzir

H
hard: difícil
high school: escolas de Ensino Médio
hoodie: moletom com capuz
how long: quanto tempo

I
intend: pretender
issue: questão

L
landscape: paisagem
lazy: preguiçoso/a

M
mall: *shopping center* (anglicismo)

N
necklace: colar
northwest: noroeste

O
opening: abertura
overall: no geral

P
pants: calça

R
relative: parente
replace: substituir

S
scarf (coloquial): devorar rapidamente
season: estação do ano
several: diversos/as
skirt: saia
slang: gíria
sneakers: tênis
staff: cetro
store: loja
sunglasses: óculos de sol

T
tank top: camiseta regata
training: treinamento
T-shirt: camiseta

U
underlying: oculto/a, subjacente

V
value: valor
vest: colete

W
weather: clima
whole: inteiro/a

CHAPTER 4

A
apricot: damasco

B
baking tray: assadeira
beans: feijão
bell pepper: pimentão
boil: ferver
bread: pão
butter: manteiga

C
carrot: cenoura
chicken: frango
chickpea: grão-de-bico
chop: picar
chunk: pedaço grande
cinnamon: canela
cold cuts: frios (presunto, mortadela, peito de peru etc.)
cumin: cominho
cup: xícara

D
dairy: laticínio
daydreaming: devanear, sonhar acordado
deseed: retirar as sementes
dinner: jantar
dish: prato
distinguish: distinguir
dried: desidratado/a, seco/a
drink: beber; bebida
drizzle: pingar, derramar um pouco

E
egg: ovo

F
farmer's market: feira
fat: gordura
fish: peixe
flavor: sabor
fry: fritar

G
glass: copo
good-humored: bem-humorado/a
ground: moído/a
guidelines: diretrizes

H
handful: punhado
harm: danificar
heat: aquecer
heritage: herança, legado
honey: mel
host: apresentar

J
juice: suco

K
kitchen: cozinha

L
lettuce: alface

M
measure: medida
meat: carne
mild: suave
milk: leite
Moroccan: marroquino/a

N
noodle: macarrão
nut: castanha, noz

O
olive oil: azeite
onion: cebola
orange: laranja
oven: forno

P
parsnip: cherívia
passionate: apaixonado/a
pasta: massa
peel: descascar
plate: prato
plump: fofinho/a, inchado/a
potato: batata
poultry: aves
powder: pó

R
refuse: recusar
rice: arroz
roast: assar
rub: esfregar

S
sauce: molho
scoop: colherada
season: temperar
serving: porção
shrimp: camarão
shy: tímido/a
skin: casca
smell: cheirar
spice: tempero

T
tablespoon: colher de sopa
teaspoon: colher de chá
tender: macio/a
tip: colocar

W
wedge: gomo
wheat: trigo

Y
youngster: jovem

CHAPTER 5

A
actually: realmente; na verdade
air: transmitir
already: já
awful: horrível

B
briefly: brevemente
bring: trazer
broadcast: transmitir; transmissão
bunch: monte (coloquial)

C
career: carreira
coin: cunhar
cornerstone: pedra fundamental
count: conde

E
enable: possibilitar
enjoyable: divertido/a

H
handheld: compacto/a, portátil
headline: manchete, título

P
play: jogar; reproduzir; tocar (instrumentos); peça de teatro

R
recorder: gravador

S
subtitle: legenda

W
win: vencer
worldwide: mundialmente

CHAPTER 6

A
achievement: conquista
among: entre
arrest: prisão

B
bright: inteligente

C
Chemistry: Química
childhood: infância
citizen: cidadão/cidadã
come up with: criar

D
degree: graduação
demand: exigência
despite: apesar de

E
earlier: anterior
earn: ganhar, obter

F
fail: reprovar
flee: fugir

G
give up: ceder
grow up: crescer

H
hide: esconder-se
high-spirited: animado/a
hope: esperança

J
Jewish: judeu/judia

L
law: Direito
length: duração

M
marvel: maravilhar-se

N
needle: agulha
novelist: romancista

P
prank: peça, brincadeira
prior: anterior, prévio/a
publisher: editora

R
release: lançamento
relinquish: abdicar, abrir mão

S
salesman: vendedor
set: estabelecer
short story: conto
speech: fala

T
trial: julgamento
trigger: desencadear

U
unabridged: integral, sem cortes

W
worried: preocupado/a

CHAPTER 7

A
alive: vivo/a
army: exército
attachment: ligação

B
bridge: ponte

C
century: século
church: igreja
coiled: enrolado/a
county seat: sede de condado
craft: artesanato

D
depth: profundidade

F
found: fundar

G
goldfield: mina de ouro

H
header: cabeçalho
helpful: útil
historian: historiador/a
honor: homenagear; honra

L
labor: mão de obra
landmark: marco, monumento
lie on: situar-se
loosely: levemente

M
muscle: músculo

O
ownership: posse, propriedade

P
paddle steamer: barco a vapor com rodas de pás

R
remain: permanecer
rubber: borracha
rule: governar

S
settlement: assentamento, colônia

shell: concha
slavery: escravidão
square: praça

CHAPTER 8

A
afraid: com medo, temeroso/a
amount: quantidade

B
ban: proibir

C
climb: escalar

D
deal: acordo
death: morte
dream: sonho

E
edict: decreto

F
firing: tiroteio

G
grid: grade, quadriculado

H
heart: coração
heavy: pesado/a
hide-and-seek: esconde-esconde
hopscotch: amarelinha
household chore: tarefa doméstica
hungry: faminto/a

I
instead: em vez de
issue: emitir

J
jump rope: pular corda
jungle gym: trepa-trepa

L
launch: lançamento
lie down: deitar-se

M
marble: bolinha de gude
monkey bars: escada horizontal (brinquedo)
mood: humor
musical chairs: dança das cadeiras

P
plaster cast: tala de gesso
prize: prêmio

R
rest: descansar
round: rodada
roundabout: gira-gira

S
seat: assento
seesaw: gangorra
shelling: bombardeio
sign: assinar
smash: esmagar
surrounded: cercado/a
swings: balanço (brinquedo)

T
toy: brinquedo
traffic jam: congestionamento
trick: truque
tug of war: cabo de guerra
tuition: aula

Learning more

Capítulo 1

The Circle

Escrito por Dave Eggers.
New York: Vintage Books, 2013.

O livro *The Circle* conta a história de Mae, uma jovem recém-formada que parece ter encontrado o emprego dos sonhos na empresa Circle, poderosa no ramo da internet: escritórios modernos, acomodação confortável, benefícios de todos os tipos. Isso tudo em troca de apenas uma coisa: a privacidade de seus funcionários, que têm a vida vigiada constantemente. A obra discute como a internet pode expor nossa intimidade.
O livro foi adaptado para o cinema em 2017 e protagonizado por Emma Watson e Tom Hanks.

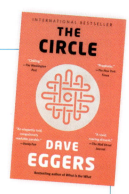

Capítulo 2

August Rush

Dirigido por Kirsten Sheridan.
Estados Unidos: Warner Bros., 2007.

O amor entre um guitarrista irlandês e uma violoncelista estadunidense é proibido pelas circunstâncias, e o bebê August, que nasce desse relacionamento, acaba sendo mandado para um orfanato. A criança, no entanto, sonha em encontrar seus pais biológicos e sabe que o caminho para alcançar seu objetivo é por meio da música, dom que herdou dos pais talentosos. O filme mostra como a música, uma das muitas formas de expressão, pode fazer a diferença na vida das pessoas.

Capítulo 3

Museu da Imigração

Nosso país é como uma colcha de retalhos costurada por imigrantes de diversos países. Para conhecer melhor a história da chegada dessas pessoas ao Brasil, visite o *site* oficial do Museu da Imigração, que mostra um pouco da difícil trajetória de italianos, japoneses, espanhóis, entre outros estrangeiros, em sua busca por melhores condições no Novo Continente. Se for possível, visite o museu físico, localizado no bairro da Mooca, na cidade de São Paulo.

Capítulo 4

Super Size Me

Dirigido por Morgan Spurlock.
Estados Unidos: Samuel Goldwyn Films, 2004.

É difícil negar a popularidade mundial de comidas do tipo *fast-food*. Mas quais seriam as consequências para nossa vida se o consumo desse tipo de alimento fosse frequente? Em seu documentário *Super Size Me*, Spurlock decide fazer o teste e se alimenta apenas desse tipo de comida por 30 dias consecutivos, com o objetivo de mostrar os efeitos negativos dessa dieta à população dos Estados Unidos, país onde os casos de obesidade são cada vez mais frequentes.

Capítulo 5

Museu do Videogame Itinerante

Você já parou para pensar como eram os primeiros consoles de *video game*? E os jogos, como eram? Se jogar *video game* é um de seus *hobbies* prediletos, visitar o Museu do Videogame Itinerante pode ser uma boa opção de entretenimento. No *site* oficial, além de ver imagens dos primeiros consoles da história, é possível também convidar o museu para visitar sua cidade. Com base nos pedidos, o museu monta uma agenda de viagens pelo país.

Capítulo 6

I Will Always Write Back

Escrito por Caitlin Alifirenka e Martin Ganda.
New York: Little, Brown Books for Young Readers, 2016.

Você já ouviu falar em jovens que trocam cartas ou *e-mails* com jovens desconhecidos de outros lugares para praticar o ato da escrita? As escolas estadunidenses incentivam os *pen pals*, como são chamados, a trocar correspondências com o intuito de abrir a mente para outras realidades. Caitlin e Martin se conhecem por meio de cartas que viajam entre os Estados Unidos e o Zimbábue, transpondo as enormes diferenças de cada um dos adolescentes: uma menina de classe média em um país desenvolvido e um garoto muito esforçado que mora em uma região pobre de um país com muitas dificuldades. O livro autobiográfico *I Will Always Write Back* é o resultado dessa relação real que mudou a vida dos dois jovens.

Capítulo 7

Ferramenta de visualização de mapas em 3-D

Há monumentos interessantes em todo o mundo, mas nem sempre é possível ir aos lugares onde eles estão para conhecê-los. Uma alternativa proporcionada pela tecnologia é visitar tais lugares através de seu computador, por meio de imagens em 360°. Para isso, pode-se utilizar uma ferramenta de exploração de mapas: nela, basta digitar o monumento que você quer ver e "arrastar" o avatar de visualização em 3-D para o mapa na tela. Você se deslumbrará com a perfeição das imagens, as vistas impressionantes e os novos lugares que irá conhecer. Algumas sugestões são: o Coliseu, em Roma, e a Muralha da China, além dos monumentos brasileiros apresentados na própria unidade.

Capítulo 8

I Am Malala

Escrito por Malala Yousafzai e Christina Lamb.
New York: Little, Brown and Company, 2013.

Malala nasceu e viveu no Paquistão até sua adolescência e sobreviveu a uma guerra violenta e a um regime autoritário graças à sua família amorosa, ao incentivo dos pais e à sua vontade de estudar. O livro autobiográfico conta a trajetória da adolescente que não desistiu de seu direito ao estudo.

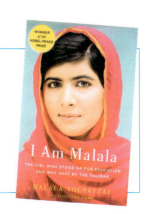

Track list

Track	Chapter	Activity	Page
1	Introduction	-	-
2	1	2	17
3	1	3	17
4	1	1	18
5	2	2	28
6	2	3	28
7	2	4	29
8	2	5	29
9	3	2, 3	43
10	4	2, 3	55
11	4	4	55
12	5	6	65
13	5	3	68
14	5	4	69
15	5	5	69
16	5	6	69
17	6	4	81
18	6	5	81
19	7	3, 4, 5	95
20	8	2, 3	107

References

ABRAMSON, Ann. *Who Was Anne Frank?* Penguin Group USA and Audible, 2009.

Britannica Concise Encyclopedia. Encyclopaedia Britannica Inc., 2008. p. 192.

Britannica Student Encyclopedia. Edinburgh: Encyclopaedia Britannica, Inc., 2012. p. 42.

BURGESS, Richard James. *The History of Music Production.* Oxford: Oxford University Press, 2014. pp. 10, 70, 151.

HORNUNG, Alfred. *Intercultural America.* Heidelberg: Winter, 2007. p. 182.

MELTZER, Brad; ELIOPOULOS, Christopher. *I Am Jane Goodall.* New York: Dial Books for Young Readers, 2016.

MISIROGLU, Gina. *The Handy Answer Book for Kids (and Parents).* Canton: Visible Ink Press, 2009. p. 112.